1

Introduction

Are you looking to break out of the same mundane routine and find a way to maximize your potential? Would you like to find true happiness beyond the daily grind finally? If so, then LIFE FORCE is your guide to realistic, enduring transformation. This book will teach you the tools and techniques required to unlock your full potential and turn your life into the thriving adventure you have always dreamed of. Unlocking your true potential will enhance your life and open the door to lasting meaningful happiness. This book will show you the path to a purposeful and rewarding life in an easy-to-read, comprehensive format. Become the master of your destiny and take the reins of your life with LIFE FORCE!

Table of Contents

Chapter 1: The Life Force

The life force is an extraordinary and invisible energy that pervades the cosmos and courses through every living being. It is an essential and cohesive power that shapes and sustains life, forging connections between all aspects of existence. Those who grasp and harmonize with the life force attain profound insights and wisdom unattainable through other means.

While the life force is referred to by different names in diverse cultures, it is most commonly associated with the Chinese philosophy of qi, the Hindu philosophy's prana, and the Japanese concept of ki. Qi embodies the invisible energy that circulates within living organisms and the universe, serving as the wellspring of all life. Prana is regarded as the vital energy within the human body, upholding life and empowering individuals to shape and govern their destinies.

The comprehension of the life force extends beyond Eastern philosophies, however, and is acknowledged across various cultures throughout history. In ancient Greece, the life force was called Pneuma and was deemed the origin of the soul and spirit. Franz Mesmer, an Austrian mystic and philosopher, employed the term "Odic force" to depict a subtle energy or life force in all living things. Whether it is the Iroquois Orenda or the Polynesian Mana, each civilization has recognized this vital force as the bedrock of existence. Despite differing names and specific definitions, they all represent the fundamental essence of life. To delve deeper into the concept of the life force, we must examine its essential components. Being attuned to the life force entails finding harmony with nature, embracing our inner wisdom, and being receptive to a power beyond ourselves that can illuminate, guide, and transform. This energy is intricately interconnected with both the physical and metaphysical realms, capable of influencing and impacting both aspects of our existence.

Furthermore, the life force is not a singular, isolated energy. It is often subdivided into distinct components based on different cultures and belief systems. In Eastern philosophies, for instance, the life force is associated with the five elements: fire, water, wood, metal, and Earth. Each element embodies a unique type of energy and is utilized to restore balance and heal physical, emotional, and spiritual afflictions. The goal is to harmonize these energies, creating an environment conducive to health and well-being.

In conclusion, the life force is a dynamic and life-giving energy that can be harnessed and employed to foster personal and spiritual growth and enhance overall well-being. We are all born with an inherent connection to this energy, and it is crucial to nurture and cultivate this relationship to fully embrace its benefits. Regardless of our cultural or belief backgrounds, understanding, aligning with, and harnessing the life force can guide us toward a more balanced, healthier, and fulfilling life.

1.1 Unleashing the Power of the Life Force

The life force possesses an incredible power that fills us with vitality and liveliness. Tapping into this divine energy unlocks its extraordinary capacity for healing, rejuvenation, and personal growth. Its profound properties strengthen our immune system, reduce inflammation, and promote physical and emotional well-being. It revitalizes our skin, slows aging, and facilitates physical regeneration. Actively engaging with the life force allows us to maintain a healthier mind and body.

Furthermore, the life force brings emotional balance and psychological well-being. Its calming and soothing qualities alleviate stress, induce relaxation, and foster a positive mindset. This heightened state of being enables greater clarity, insight, and realization of our potential. It opens doors to expanded problem-solving abilities and heightened creativity. By accessing this energy, we tap into increased levels of innovation, making even the most daunting tasks more manageable.

The life force is an unparalleled resource for those seeking a more fulfilling existence. By harnessing its incredible power, we unlock superhuman capabilities, gain profound self-awareness, clarify our goals, improve our physical and mental well-being, and boost our energy levels. Moreover, the life force naturally enhances our energy levels. By unblocking our energy channels and allowing the life force to flow freely, we can easily augment the energy in our lives, resulting in improved productivity and reduced fatigue. Accessing the life force becomes an extraordinary tool for maximizing our potential.

To avoid succumbing to the limitations imposed by the physical laws of nature, we need proper management of the life force. These laws include the aging process with all its adverse side effects.

Reflecting on my life, I have personally experienced the feeling that life has taken its toll and witnessed a decline in vitality after a period of greatness. For instance, I was in India recovering from a long and stressful phase. I anticipated a smooth process, which did not unfold as planned. Instead, I deteriorated even further from this long and stressful phase. It must have been inevitable in middle age, but I could not accept such a decline as my fate. I refused to believe that acceptance was my only option. I was convinced that I had much more to accomplish in this lifetime than going with the flow of aging. I wanted to feel alive and vibrant like a teenager with a whole life in front of them. I wanted to participate in all kinds of activities like sports without the age-related issues most people have in older age. Feeling young is bliss, and even on this day, I want to exploit that as much as possible. While I intended to recover in India, I encountered unforeseen challenges and a lack of tranquility I sought. This eventually led to a severe bout of flu, and I had to adjust to create a facade of the comfort I was accustomed to in the West.

As the life force gradually drained from my body, I yearned for my younger self's vitality and vibrant energy. Despite reaching an age when physical decline is expected, I firmly believed it was not an inevitable fate for me. While confined to bed for several days, I found an Instagram post with the caption "Vibe Check." It featured a crossword puzzle where the first word seen reflected one's current state. The word that caught my attention was "healing." Accompanying the image was a message: "The best remedy lies in surrendering completely and attentively listening to the messages of the body." This realization struck me profoundly. Both posts were shared by Teal Swan, a well-known spiritual teacher.

Subsequently, I discovered a video on Gaia.com titled "Egyptian Postures of Power" featuring Jason Quitt. He shared his story of breaking three vertebrae in his spine due to an unfortunate fall but could walk again after three months through intensive meditation. At that moment, everything fell into place for me. I simply needed to cultivate my life force energy—a practice that should have been initiated earlier but appeared impossible due to circumstances. There was no better timing than where I was at that moment, and a few hours later, after actively cultivating my life force as I paced restlessly in anticipation of dinner, I noticed a surge in my energy levels. The flu gradually faded into the background. My spice for life had been reignited. The downward spiral of aging was thankfully left behind. I felt blessed, even euphoric. The following day, I embarked on a three-hour car ride to my next destination, feeling enthusiastic, youthful, and vibrant again! This experience marked a significant milestone in my life, laying the foundation for writing this book, "LIFE FORCE." As the title suggests, "Living to Your Maximum Potential and Achieving True Happiness." This is an invitation that I'd like to share with the world. I don't want you to suffer due to lacking life force but to participate in life with maximum potential, with the methods for cultivating the life force described in this book.

1.2 Harnessing the Life Force for Healing

Our world is intricately woven together by a profound life force that permeates every facet of existence, from the minuscule particles that make up matter to the colossal galaxies that dot the cosmos. This invisible force flows through our very being, connecting us intimately with the vastness of the universe. Astonishingly, despite its immeasurable significance, modern science and medicine have ignored it mainly to recognize its true power, resulting in overcrowded hospitals and treatments that often fall short due to a lack of comprehensive understanding. While medical professionals tirelessly perform incredible feats, considerable room remains for improvement. By integrating the concept of the life force into the fabric of common knowledge, we have the potential to alleviate the global reliance on medications and conventional medical interventions.

Since the beginning of the Industrial Revolution, our reliance on technology has grown exponentially, often portraying it as our ultimate savior in the face of adversity. We delight in the comforts provided by the widespread availability of supermarkets and the progress in modern healthcare. However, beneath the surface, a yearning persists within many of us, a longing for a more profound comprehension of our well-being. Regrettably, the general approach in medical practice often revolves around treating symptoms rather than addressing the underlying causes of illnesses. Hence, we must comprehensively understand our intricate bodily mechanisms and processes. By attuning ourselves to the innate wisdom of our bodies and harnessing the inherent power of the life force coursing through us, we can prevent diseases and sustain optimal health. Yet, in a world preoccupied with external influences and instant gratification, many individuals search for happiness outside of themselves, relying on external factors to shape their well-being. Whether it is through altering our physical appearance or seeking ways to improve our health, we frequently turn to medical professionals, cosmetic procedures, medications, or topical treatments. But what if we could initiate transformative changes from within?

As I reflect upon my journey, memories of my encounters with doctors during my formative years resurface. Filled with hope and yearning for relief from the discomfort and afflictions that plagued me, I sought remedies and cures. Yet, disappointingly, the solutions offered were often mere painkillers, providing temporary respite from the symptoms but failing to address the underlying causes. The dissatisfaction within me stemmed from realizing that these experts lacked a profound understanding of my specific ailments. How can it be that even today, a significant gap exists in our collective knowledge of the intricate workings of the human body? Driven by this discontent, I embarked on a personal quest, delving deeper into research and exploration, pushing the boundaries of healing into uncharted territories.

In this profound journey, I found a clear link between the mind, body, and spirit—a trio of interconnected elements that play a vital role in holistic well-being.

Unraveling the mysteries of illness and its origins, I excavated a profound truth: true healing lies not merely in treating the physical symptoms but in managing the mental and emotional landscapes that underpin our existence. By peering into the depths of our innermost selves and addressing the core of our being, we can halt the progression of diseases and restore balance and vitality. Thus, I embarked on a transformative inward journey during those challenging times, seeking comfort and healing when external alternatives seemed scarce. Through years of practice, dedication, and unwavering belief, I regained my vitality and acquired a profound understanding of the life force and how to harness its potent energy for healing.

In the following pages, I will share the insights and wisdom I gained from my odyssey. From my struggles with a hernia, asthma, and various skin conditions such as psoriasis and eczema to the burdens of rheumatism and autoimmune disorders, I have overcome these afflictions without relying solely on medical intervention or external remedies. Instead, I have learned to tap into the boundless reservoir of the life force energy within each of us. The knowledge and techniques presented in this book can transform our lives and countless

others who seek to unlock the healing
power of the life force.

Chapter 2: The Profound Impact of Aging and Disease on Psychological Well-being

The psychological effects of aging and disease profoundly influence an individual's quality of life. The process of aging and the start of illness can gradually deplete one's life force, leading to devastating consequences. As individuals age, they encounter many physical and mental changes that can significantly affect their health and well-being. These psychological effects often manifest as reduced mental and physical capabilities, an increased vulnerability to stress and depression, and a degrading sense of control over one's life force.

Although the psychological effects of aging and disease may differ from person to person, individuals may share everyday experiences. Feelings of loneliness, fear, anxiety, sadness, hopelessness, and depression can emerge as the body undergoes weakening. Individuals may become disheartened and dispirited as confidence diminishes, mainly as their roles and responsibilities decrease. The gradual decline in physical functioning leaves individuals more vulnerable to physical pain and limitations in their activities, which brings a heightened awareness of their own mortality and diminished capabilities. For those grappling with life-threatening illnesses like cancer, the burden of such conditions can often result in a deep sense of depression.

Undoubtedly, depression is one of the most prevalent psychological effects accompanying aging and disease. Feelings of helplessness, sadness, hopelessness, worthlessness, and exhaustion converge to contribute to the development and intensification of depression. Moreover, individuals may grapple with a pervasive sense of losing control over their lives, leaving them with a perceived inability to change their circumstances positively. Additionally, the experience of grief and feelings of isolation may further worsen psychological distress. During this journey, letting go of attachments can serve as a helpful catalyst for personal growth and healing. Reflecting on the past can evoke emotions and associations with how things used to be, such as the vibrancy and invincibility often felt during the age of seventeen. "It is a common Dutch saying that "Je bent zo oud als je je voelt," which means "you're only as old as you feel," emphasizing the psychological perception of age."

Based on my personal experiences, growing older is different from the linear progression it is generally perceived to be. I have frequently felt and appeared more aged. Fortunately, I can return to my younger self through life force cultivation, accompanied by renewed energy and vitality. Experiencing the emotions and associations with how things used to be in the moment. In other words, has nothing to do with age per se.

Like a regular gym routine, rejuvenation is a life force method that improves with consistent practice. It entails nurturing and maintaining the body in a healthy state. Becoming younger encompasses external appearance and internal revitalization. I have talked with numerous individuals about their views on aging. Surprisingly, many still claim to have no qualms about growing older. Perhaps they have lost unrealistic expectations and prefer to avoid making false promises to themselves. It's as if they don't believe in rejuvenation anymore.

Another well-known Dutch saying, "Ouder worden komt met gebreken" (Growing older comes with ailments), suggests that life can become more demanding as one ages, often accompanied by various physical discomforts. However, rejuvenation and vitality are intrinsically tied to a sense of youthfulness. How empowering it is to effortlessly climb stairs or run without any limitations! As the years pass, these once-simple tasks can become demanding trials. Nevertheless, when the life force is harnessed and channeled appropriately, it has the potential to restore and revitalize our bodies, resulting in a more youthful and healthier appearance. Instead of witnessing the aging process unfold before our eyes in front of the mirror, we can consciously embark on a transformative journey through the cultivation of our life forces each time we face our reflection.

2.1 Aging and the Impact of Stress

Aging is a natural process that affects all living beings and has captivated scientific researchers for many years. Extensive studies have shed light on the intricate mechanisms underlying aging and the development of age-related diseases.

To comprehend aging, it is crucial to delve into its fundamental biology. Cells continuously replicate and generate new cells to replace old ones. However, this process slows down as humans age, resulting in less efficient cell and tissue reproduction. Moreover, aging cells become more prone to coding errors, leading to diseases that further deteriorate the aging body.

In the quest to unravel the mysteries of aging, scientists have investigated specific markers in the body that indicate changes associated with aging. These markers include hormone levels, oxidative stress and inflammation markers, cellular markers, and gene expression.

Researchers have attempted to understand these markers' role in the aging process. For instance, elevated oxidative stress and inflammation levels are linked to an increased risk of age-related diseases such as Alzheimer's and diabetes. Additionally, reduced levels of hormones such as testosterone and estrogen are associated with accelerated aging.

In addition to exploring the biological aspects of aging, researchers have examined the impact of lifestyle choices on aging.

Numerous studies have revealed correlations between lifestyle factors, such as diet and exercise, and a decreased risk of age-related diseases. Adopting a healthy diet rich in nutritious foods and regular exercise can slow or delay aging and mitigate age-related diseases. However, it is essential to note that other factors may contribute to maintaining a youthful lifestyle.

Scientists have also investigated potential ways to reverse the aging process. While there is no scientific cure for aging, at least not in the public sector, research is ongoing. Scientists are exploring methods to restore damaged or malfunctioning cells using stem cell therapy or gene editing techniques. Additionally, they are studying how to manipulate gene expression to slow down or reverse aging.

Aging is a multifaceted process that scientists still strive to fully comprehend.

Research has provided valuable insights into the biology of aging and the lifestyle choices that can promote healthy aging. Furthermore, it is evident from my research that aging and disease stem from a lack of life force. Considering that all matter and physical manifestations are byproducts of universal energy, it becomes clear that life cannot be sustained without it. By scrutinizing the topic of aging and disease, we find that stress emerges as a significant factor. Stress disrupts the flow of life force, making it more challenging for cells to reproduce.

Stress plays a significant role in physical and mental changes, accelerating aging. Consider two individuals of the same age. Let's say a twin, one who has led a relatively calm and relaxing life, and another who has experienced extreme stress. The individual who has lived stressfully would likely appear older. But how does this happen? Stress creates tension within the body, causing muscles to tighten. When we experience stress, our bodies release cortisol, which prepares us for fight or flight. Consequently, muscles tense up in anticipation of action, often leading to discomfort and pain if not relieved.

In addition to the physical response, stress can cause psychological tension, leading to muscle tension. This can occur when we feel overwhelmed, struggle to cope with constant demands, or attempt to ward off feelings of depression and anxiety. Over time, the tension becomes ingrained, akin to an involuntary muscle-tightening reflex.

An analogy can be drawn between tension within the body and a dam. The dam represents a blockage that disrupts the natural flow of vital energy, impeding the circulation of nutrients and minerals. Tension in our bodies hinders the proper flow of life force. Just as an open dam can cause flooding, the barrier or tightness within our bodies hinders the flow of life force and can lead to chronic illness and disease.

Therefore, it is essential to release tension periodically. Failure to release tension can result in becoming easily agitated over trivial matters. Engaging in activities such as relaxation, massage, sexual intimacy, meditation, yoga, and spending time in nature can aid in releasing tension and allowing the energy to flow smoothly.

When tapping into and producing the life force, it is crucial to remember that the relaxation of the body is integral to maintaining the correct flow of energy.

2.2 Exploring the Three Primary Causes of Aging

Looking back on my life, I realize it has been quite adventurous. For instance, I have moved more than 30 times, including a period of homelessness. Although this dynamic was necessary for my personal growth, it allowed me to discover a great deal. One of these discoveries is that everything in the external world is in constant motion. Nothing in life remains fixed. Situations, objects, material possessions, colleagues, friends, and romantic partners eventually come and go. Even our bodies are in constant motion, with cells constantly being recreated and broken down until we are reborn again. We can assume that life is an endless cycle. However, life can be stressful if we cling to certain things, like building a house of cards that can collapse with the slightest touch. This reminds me of the Tibetan sand mandalas created and then destroyed by

Tibetan Buddhists. These mandalas are traditionally made as a ceremonial and meditative practice.

Monks use colored sand to create complex geometric patterns and symbols representing the cosmos and life. Creating a Tibetan sand mandala is meticulous and requires great patience and precision. Creating a mandala can take several days to weeks, depending on the complexity of its design.

The sand is collected and usually poured into a river or ocean to spread the positive energy it contains. Once the mandala is completed, it is often displayed for admiration. Subsequently, the mandala is ceremonially destroyed. This symbolizes the temporariness of life and the teaching of detachment.

The creation and destruction of sand mandalas is a profound spiritual practice that helps Buddhists understand the impermanence of material forms and the art of letting go. It serves as a reminder of the transience of everything in life and the inherent transformation of existence. Holding onto familiar patterns within and outside ourselves ultimately leads to despondency, depression, aging, or disease. A healthy lifestyle, therefore, is to let go of attachments, cultivate, and flow with the current of the life force.

Throughout my life, I have experienced many phenomena, including depression, aging, and disease, and have come to realize that the three primary causes of illness or aging are influenced by three significant factors: stress, identity, and our relationship with time. While these factors are interconnected, stress is generally recognized as the primary cause of aging and disease. However, delving deeper into the other two elements, particularly when considering the concept of life force, is crucial. By examining these three primary factors, we can better understand their impact on our bodies and explore how the life force can help manage them.

As we delve into the complexities of aging and the impact of stress. Our lifestyles are increasingly defined by financial pressures and deadlines, resulting in unprecedented stress and anxiety levels. This stress infiltrates every aspect of our lives, from relationships and daily responsibilities to how we perceive ourselves.

Prioritizing work over our well-being has become the norm, but it comes at a cost to our mental and physical health. The relentless monotony and high expectations of our daily routines gradually corrupt our ability to think independently and take control of our lives.

Modern society places significant emphasis on success, often measured by material possessions such as wealth and power. The pressure to perform can lead to low self-esteem and unhealthy perfectionism, ultimately contributing to depression, anxiety, and burnout. The constant influx of personal and societal information can further disrupt our mental balance and overwhelm us, with technology deeply ingrained in our lives, enabling constant connectivity and informing us about the ever-changing world. However, this dependency on technology can sometimes become burdensome and overwhelming. We find ourselves stressed, overwhelmed, and trapped in an endless cycle of multitasking rather than being fully present in the moment.

The pressure to succeed in our personal and professional endeavors can be challenging. It's important to remember that our happiness should take precedence over external achievements.

Stress is a significant factor associated with aging and disease. While stress has become normalized in our modern lives, our inability to cope can lead to various physical and mental health problems, almost like an involuntary tightening of the muscles, which blocks the life force flow. While it may not be possible to completely eliminate stress, we can tap into our life force and relax the body to find balance.

Identity: Identity is a complex concept that profoundly influences physical, emotional, mental, and spiritual well-being. From a scientific perspective, our identity shapes our thoughts, emotions, and interactions with the world. Emotions trigger hormonal changes in our bodies, affecting our physical well-being. Positive emotions like joy and contentment release oxytocin, promoting relaxation and reducing stress. On the other hand, negative emotions such as anxiety and stress can trigger the release of cortisol, which has detrimental effects on our physical health if cortisol levels remain elevated for prolonged periods.

Identity also plays a role in how we age and the rate at which we age, influencing our vulnerability to certain diseases and mortality rates. Our beliefs and self-perceptions can program our bodies to age and appear older. For example, our physical appearance may reflect a strong identification with a particular period or role. I am a grandmother or father, and I am 45 or 60. These thoughts or titles can program our bodies if we believe in these roles or identities. In other words, our identity shapes our perception of reality and can influence the experiences and opportunities we attract.

Another fascinating concept and the primary cause of aging is our relationship with time.

Time: Albert Einstein introduced the concept of the relativity of time, which he published in a paper titled "On the Electrodynamics of Moving Bodies" in 1905, suggesting that time is not a fixed constant but varies depending on the observer's position and velocity. This means that time is subjective to the observer. For instance, if a spacecraft travels close to the speed of light, time would pass more slowly for those aboard the spaceship than for those on Earth. Aging is not solely determined by the elapsed time, as people age at different rates. Instead, it depends on how individuals relate to time, which is also connected to their identity. If time is relative, then aging must also be close.

In a society that emphasizes speed and efficiency, we often rush through our schedules, leading to exhaustion and straining our biological systems. The pressure to keep up with the world's pace can make us fixated on time and its limitations. This pursuit of speed is evident in modern media and social platforms, where rapid imagery and a competitive atmosphere dominate our attention.

Time is a complex concept closely intertwined with prolonged tension within the body and identity. If time is merely an illusion, and our perception of it is relative, we can consciously step out of its limitations.

Reflecting on my life, I notice that time speeds up significantly, making it nearly impossible to keep up with the ever-changing world. My inner nature, on the other hand, tends to move at a much slower pace. However, when I listen to and trust my intuition, slowing down allows me to disconnect from the fast-paced whirlwind of the outside world and tune into a different frequency.

The relentless acceleration surrounding us often leads to nowhere, much like the daily commute where people are stuck in traffic jams. In contrast, when I embrace a state of deceleration, I also age more gracefully. I can visibly witness myself growing older daily by constantly rushing like most people do. But I need a different lifestyle, similar of those in remoted areas.

It becomes crucial to examine our relationship with time and align ourselves with our inner nature, where our life force energy flows freely.

By relaxing, releasing time constraints, and consciously tapping into our life force, we can positively influence our well-being and slow or even reverse aging.

In summary, stress is recognized as the primary cause of aging and disease. Our modern lifestyles, filled with financial pressures, deadlines, and societal expectations, contribute to unprecedented stress and anxiety levels. Prioritizing work over well-being takes a toll on our mental and physical health, leading to burnout, depression, and low self-esteem. The constant influx of information and technology further overwhelms us, disrupting our mental balance and ability to be present.

Identity profoundly influences our well-being. Our thoughts, emotions, and interactions with the world are shaped by our identity. Positive emotions release oxytocin, promoting relaxation, while negative emotions trigger the release of cortisol, which is detrimental to our physical health. Our beliefs and self-perceptions can program our bodies to age and appear older, shaping our experiences and opportunities.

The concept of time is explored through the relativity of time proposed by Albert

Einstein. Time is subjective, and individuals relate to it differently. In a fast-paced society, rushing through schedules and fixating on time can exhaust us and strain our biological systems. Our perception of time is closely connected to prolonged tension within the body, consciousness or identity. By stepping out of time limitations, slowing down, and aligning with our inner nature, we can positively influence our well-being and slow or reverse aging. We must manage stress, cultivate a positive identity, and redefine our relationship with time. We can gracefully enhance our well-being and age by tapping into our life force energy, relaxing, and releasing attachment to external pressures. Understanding the three primary causes of aging empowers us to embrace a healthier lifestyle and unlock the potential of the life force within us.

2.3 The Mirror

Mirrors play an indispensable role in our society today. They are omnipresent in bathrooms, fitting rooms, fitness centers, ballrooms, and bedrooms. We also encounter mirrors in the form of makeup mirrors, selfie cameras, and reflections in windows. It's nearly impossible to avoid seeing our reflection in these mirrors.

Looking good and presentable is essential for most of us in various settings such as dates, work, appointments, and family gatherings. Therefore, a mirror can be seen as an indicator of our current appearance. When we look at ourselves in the mirror, we may perceive ourselves as unattractive on some days, with bad skin and bags under our eyes, or we may appear tired with messy hair that needs fixing. On the other hand, there are days when we look fantastic. Regardless, the mirror can be our biggest fan and our greatest critic. It often sets the tone for how we approach the rest of our day. Looking good can significantly boost our confidence. We all recognize that our bodies undergo physical changes, and no two days are the same. Therefore, time and aging are relative concepts. The speed at which we age or rejuvenate differs for each individual. Some people appear better as they grow older, often when they have undergone a personal transformation within themselves. As we see with identity. Signs of aging can manifest rapidly, especially when we are under prolonged stress and not aligned with our inner nature. These changes become noticeable when we look at ourselves in the mirror. I have witnessed my transformation in front of the mirror countless times, sometimes within minutes. Taking conscious breaks from the hectic pace of life, such as going on a beach vacation or relaxing at a resort, can lead to immediate improvements in our appearance. Relaxation facilitates the flow of life force energy, which becomes evident in our body and mind, allowing us to embrace life with vitality. Therefore, a mirror can indicate our current state and provide insights into what our body needs. Taking good care of our bodies is crucial for enhancing our overall quality of life.

Standing in front of the mirror, I now approach my reflection differently. I vividly remember being 19 years old and feeling shocked when I saw my first wrinkle etched on my forehead in the mirror. I was unhappy and feared it would worsen, signaling my youth's fading. I felt upset and knew I had to take action to prevent further wrinkles. Intuitively, I started working with life force energy, and to my amazement, the wrinkle vanished entirely within a week. Since then, I have used life force energy for facelifting, a natural method described in this book. Even now, nearing the age of 40, I have no wrinkles at all.

Therefore, a mirror can be seen as both an indicator and a tool for rejuvenation. When we notice wrinkles or bags under our eyes in the mirror, for example, it signals the need for practical solutions. It all revolves around harnessing the power of life force energy while relaxing the skin tissue. A mirror can be a helpful tool for those who wish to age gracefully. I have witnessed my aging process in front of the mirror and successfully reversed it many times. The previous chapter highlighted the Three Primary Causes of Aging, with stress as the number one factor. Like stress, wrinkles often result from prolonged tension in the facial muscles caused by repetitive facial expressions. Over time, we become accustomed to these tension areas, considering them normal and resulting in a marked appearance. For instance, someone who frequently expresses anger may appear angry even when they are not consciously feeling that way. This is because their body has adapted to that state. This phenomenon is often observed in mothers who frequently correct their children, with their corresponding facial expressions leaving an imprint on their faces. While there is the option of injecting fillers or opting for Botox, which I don't oppose if someone chooses that path. Alternative methods are available, such as face yoga, massage, or Natural Facelifting, described in this book. Our reflection in the mirror shows us our physical appearance and provides insight into what needs to be addressed within ourselves. As an energy therapist in one of my professions, I always tell my clients that if they can feel or perceive something that exists, they can change it by definition. Everything is energy, as affirmed by the principles of quantum physics. When we look in the mirror, we can also feel the tension areas and wrinkles on our faces. Using simple life force methods and the techniques outlined in this book, we can localize these areas within ourselves and effectively address them. By harnessing our life force energies, we can quickly diminish wrinkles or reduce the appearance of bags under our eyes. Each time we encounter a mirror, we approach it with a newfound understanding. When we notice something we dislike about ourselves, we now possess the knowledge and tools to address it.

2.4 The Multifaceted Nature of Beauty

In our modern society, beauty has evolved far beyond its superficial definitions and is now recognized as an essential aspect of our life force. Beauty has transformed into an art form, a means of expression, and even a status symbol. Its power is so profound that it can act as a golden ticket, effortlessly opening doors of opportunity. Individuals blessed with attractive features often enjoy a more comprehensive range of job prospects and a larger pool of potential partners. While the allure of physical attractiveness can be captivating and exhilarating, we must take a moment to reflect on how we truly perceive ourselves.

When we stand before the mirror, do we genuinely appreciate the unique qualities that define us, or does our attention gravitate towards perceived imperfections? Do we fall into a sense of victimhood when confronted with the inevitability of aging, or do we embrace this natural progression of life? Regardless of age, we must refrain from excessively emphasizing societal beauty standards. Instead, we should enhance our physical appearance to align with our authentic selves. By tapping into our innate vitality and beauty, we can adopt a new approach that differs from relying on fillers, Botox, or plastic surgery.

The significance of beauty should not go unnoticed or underappreciated. It is often taken for granted and rarely discussed openly. Upon studying various forms of marketing, including Instagram, I have observed the lack of explicit mention of beauty. It is as if the concept of beauty is an unspeakable topic that we all unconsciously take for granted. When creating successful content, the focus is usually on educational, entertaining, promotional, or inspiring aspects rather than beauty itself, even though many of the most successful content pieces incorporate an element of beauty. Nowadays, it has become trendy to use beauty filters, and nearly everyone participates in this trend. This indicates that beauty does hold a certain level of importance. However, imagine how incredible it would be to naturally achieve and maintain a beautiful appearance.

A fulfilling life should not be measured solely by financial wealth but by attaining a harmonious balance in all aspects of our existence, particularly our physical well-being. We are constantly driven to pursue perfection or seek something better. We yearn for improved relationships, financial stability, enhanced skills, physical fitness, and more. Beauty is just one facet of the intricate game of life in which we actively engage. It originates from an inner wellspring of happiness and contentment. Good looks often emanate from individuals who radiate joy despite life's hardships. Those who have freed themselves from the constraints of old habits and societal conditioning tend to possess a magnetism that transcends age. As we learned, the concept of aging is, in fact, relative, and so is beauty. It is crucial to cultivate a genuine sense of beauty within ourselves. Our main goal should not be impressing others but rather confirming our self-worth, especially when looking in a mirror.

Our thoughts wield immense power over our overall well-being, and we must move beyond negative emotions to cultivate personal success. Natural Facelifting or Bodyshaping are life force methods that surpass reliance on artificial enhancements such as chemicals, surgical procedures, and other external factors. They represent a new form of art that shapes our bodies through energetic intent. By wholeheartedly embracing the life force, we can effectively reverse the effects of aging and enhance our natural beauty. Embracing this innate force within us and tapping into our inherent vitality allows us to unlock the secrets of timeless allure. Consequently, we discover that true beauty is not an elusive ideal to be pursued but a manifestation of our inner radiance.

Chapter 3: Unleashing the Power of the Vital Life Force

Recently, many individuals have been drawn towards alternative methods to enhance their vital life force, seeing them as complementary approaches to traditional medicine. These methods offer unique benefits and have the potential to significantly contribute to overall well-being. Before we dive deeper into these practices, it is essential to provide additional information. As mentioned in the previous chapter, my innate connection to life force energy and lifelong meditation practice have been deeply ingrained within me since childhood. Rather than something that was taught to me, these aspects are inherent inclinations, which some spiritual circles attribute to having an old soul. My vivid memories of past lives further solidify this belief, one of which involved being a great master along the Silk Road, a historical trade route spanning China, India, and Persia (present-day Iran). Such abilities often manifest naturally within us because we have already undergone the lessons associated with them in previous incarnations. It is as if our inherent talents and knowledge are carried over from these past experiences, just as the musical genius of Mozart transcends time. Although a comprehensive exploration of this topic could fill an entire book, it is best saved for another occasion.

Throughout my quest for a comprehensive understanding of life, I have maintained an unwavering belief in the existence of the supernatural, as if the answers to life's mysteries were intricately woven into the fabric of my being. During my formative years, I spent countless hours perusing libraries and devouring books on various subjects, including quantum mechanics, metaphysics, Theosophy, mythology, ufology, history, occultism, parapsychology, and many more. I relentlessly sought the elusive answers that would satisfy my thirst for knowledge. Yet, more often than not, I faced dead ends, as if the stream of information stopped at a certain point, unable to transcend certain boundaries. The data would abruptly cease, leaving me enigmatic fragments that seemed to venture into wholly different dimensions. This paradox is vividly exemplified in occult or religious contexts. It demands profound contemplation and digestion, resembling a mental and spiritual feast that requires prolonged introspection. To transcend, one has to go inward.

For example, quote: "Theosophy holds that every man, from the first ray of primitive divine thought down to the last speck of human mud, is entitled to the fullest intellectual and spiritual development possible. Each is a part of the divine whole, inseparable from the rest of that whole, whether in heaven or on Earth, and because each is of the whole, the whole is in each, and every smallest particle contains the germ of the whole." From the book "The Key to Theosophy" by H.P. Blavatsky. Meaning: Regardless of background or circumstances, everyone has the right to reach their highest intellectual and spiritual development potential. The belief is that every individual is an integral part of the divine unity, interconnected with all other beings, whether in heavenly realms or on Earth. This interconnectedness means that the essence of the whole is present within each individual, and even the tiniest particle contains the potential for the entire divine existence. The best way to describe it comes from the word gnosis.

The word "gnosis" originates from Greek and carries various meanings depending on the context. In its most general sense, "gnosis" refers to knowledge or understanding, particularly of a spiritual or esoteric nature. It denotes deep, intuitive, and experiential learning beyond intellectual comprehension. Gnosis is often associated with direct personal insight, illumination, or revelation that brings about a profound understanding of oneself, the divine, or the nature of existence. In spiritual and philosophical traditions, gnosis is often linked to pursuing inner wisdom and a deeper understanding of spiritual truths or mysteries rather than relying on external sources. It emphasizes the transformative power of knowledge gained through direct experience or inner awakening. With gnosis, these texts become logical.

In religious contexts, where ethical norms and values are exalted, supporters sometimes engage in conflicts driven by differing beliefs (ego) despite contextual similarities. The scripture, "You shall not take vengeance or bear a grudge against the sons of your own people, but you shall love your neighbor as yourself: I am the LORD" (Leviticus 19:18), captures this very essence. These answers, I came to realize, could only be unearthed by transcending the confines of our everyday reality—by going beyond the limitations of the mind and its conceptual thinking or gnosis. I delved further into my meditative practices and began experimenting extensively with life force energy, integrating its power into my daily existence. It was as if I possessed an innate understanding that the supernatural was intricately interwoven with the life force, and I yearned to uncover more about this profound connection.

The transformative effects I experienced were nothing short of astounding. I witnessed a remarkable surge of energy within myself, enabling me to endure more extended periods and accomplish once-impossible feats. Even to this day, I continue to exhibit extraordinary vitality and athleticism. While the passage of time has naturally brought about a more relaxed state of being, alleviating the need for constant exertion, I still maintain a remarkable physical shape. The sheer joy derived from an active lifestyle becomes even more pronounced when one's body willingly cooperates. Of course, it is essential to acknowledge that my life isn't exceptional, filled with its fair share of challenges and stressful moments.

Paradoxically, despite my trials, I have retained a remarkably youthful appearance—an outcome that defies conventional wisdom, especially considering the demands of my lifestyle. This is precisely why I regard life force energy as the "eighth wonder of the world" and feel compelled to write a comprehensive book on the subject.

So that you, too, can experience the world's eight wonders. The influence of the life force on my body and overall well-being has been profound, and I believe this knowledge should be shared with the world.

While the concept of life force has existed for ages, I have developed a unique approach that aligns harmoniously with the present era. My naturally independent-minded disposition has led me to embark on a personal journey, charting my own path and often giving rise to innovative ideas. However, I must emphasize the importance of individual research and exploration to discover what resonates best. It is vital to approach these practices with a healthy dose of skepticism while remaining attuned to one's intuition. This chapter will explore other methods that are based on the life force.

Reiki: Rooted in Eastern philosophies, Reiki is a natural healing system that focuses on the life force energy present in all living beings. Skilled practitioners touch different body parts gently to restore balance and augment the natural flow of energies coursing through the recipient. This holistic approach addresses physical ailments and alleviates emotional stress, fostering overall well-being by harmonizing the connections between the mind, body, and spirit.

Tai Chi: Founded upon the principles of Chinese medicine, Tai Chi is an ancient martial art that has evolved into a graceful and meditative practice. Characterized by slow, rhythmic movements performed with focused intention and synchronized with deep breathing, Tai Chi cultivates balance, improves circulation, enhances flexibility, reduces stress, boosts energy levels, and even alleviates chronic pain or depression. It engenders a profound sense of tranquility, infusing one's being with a harmonious flow of life force energy.

Acupuncture: In ancient China, acupuncture was a therapeutic technique that involved unblocking and harmonizing the body's energy flow, known as Qi (pronounced "chee"). By delicately inserting thin needles into specific points on the body, called acupuncture points, practitioners sought to restore the natural equilibrium of Qi, thereby alleviating stress, anxiety, illnesses, and physical pain. This practice facilitates converting the body's innate energy flow, promoting balance and supporting the vital life force.

Chakra Healing: Chakra healing represents an ancient holistic approach that involves working with the life force energy present within the body. The human body is believed to possess seven distinct energy centers, known as chakras, positioned along the spine. Each chakra corresponds to specific body areas and influences various physical, mental, emotional, and spiritual well-being aspects. Through meditation, energy work, and balancing techniques, chakra healing aims to clear blockages and restore the harmonious flow of life force energy throughout the chakra system, promoting overall vitality and holistic wellness.

Tantra and Kundalini Practices: Tantra is an ancient spiritual discipline that strives to attain inner peace and equilibrium by harmonizing physical and spiritual energies. It encompasses various practices, including meditation, breathwork, chanting, and body postures known as asanas. Tantra acknowledges the presence of a dormant power known as Kundalini, which resides at the base of the spine. Through tantric practices, such as Kundalini awakening, individuals seek to activate and channel this potent life force energy, unlocking transformative experiences and spiritual growth.

Pranayama: Pranayama is a breath control technique used in yoga to increase the life force or prana that flows through the body. This technique involves deep, rhythmic breathing, breath retention, and alternate nostril breathing, which cleanses energy channels, creates balance and harmony, and activates internal organs. Pranayama helps strengthen the immune system, achieve inner peace, and improve overall well-being.

Yoga is another ancient practice that enhances the life force by allowing individuals to access their inner energy and strengthen their connection with the natural world. Through mindful movement, asanas (yoga postures), and pranayama, yoga increases body awareness, reduces stress, and helps energy flow freely, improving vitality and creating a stronger connection to the life force.

Detoxing: Detoxing promotes body balance, optimal health, and energy by improving digestion, reducing inflammation, eliminating toxins, and improving circulation. It can also improve sleep, mental clarity, and overall well-being. In another chapter, we will delve into detoxing extensively and how it can benefit the life force flow.

The Life Force Body: Finally, unleashing the power of the life force can be done through the chakras and the skin, resulting in vitality and rejuvenation.

The following chapters will explore some of these practices, their principles, techniques, and potential benefits. By sharing these insights, I hope to inspire you to embark on your own journey of enhancing and harnessing the vital life force within you. Remember, proper understanding and mastery of these practices come from direct experience. Let us embark on this transformative exploration together, nurturing the boundless potential within each of us.

3.1 Discovering the Power of Life Force through Pranayama

The life force, or prana, holds immense potential to enhance significantly various aspects of our lives. Whether we seek healing from physical ailments, rejuvenation of our body and mind, improved physical fitness, relief from pain and discomfort, spiritual connection and growth, or even the ability to reduce our dependence on food, tapping into the life force can bring about profound changes in our well-being and experiences.

To fully understand and utilize the power of the life force, we need to become intimately familiar with its sensations and how it operates within us. Just like our muscles have memory and respond automatically to certain stimuli, our bodies instinctively activate the life force when necessary. For example, in moments of intense pain, after experiencing a fall, or even when we accidentally come into contact with something hot, such as spilling hot tea on ourselves, the vital life force is automatically engaged to protect and heal us.

We become conscious of its presence by becoming familiarized with the sensations and feelings associated with the life force. Our bodies learn to utilize this force intentionally, further expanding its beneficial effects on our physical, mental, and spiritual well-being.

Let us now embark on a pranayama practice, or life force breathing, to deepen our understanding and connection with the life force. Pranayama can be likened to a balloon that requires air to inflate and maintain its shape. Similarly, pranayama aims to strengthen our breath and grant us mastery over our vital energy, prana, or life force through specific respiratory exercises. By consciously engaging in pranayama, we effectively harness the life force as a valuable tool for our overall well-being.

Without proper management and awareness, the life force can deplete, leaving us feeling drained and fatigued. This depletion is similar to a deflated balloon that loses its vitality. However, by engaging in pranayama practices, we metaphorically inflate the balloon with life force, filling ourselves with life-giving breaths and expanding our capacity to live a vibrant and energized life.

It is important to note that the first pranayama exercise we will explore is not recommended for individuals with heart conditions. If you are interested in attempting this exercise, consult an expert or perform it under the supervision of a qualified practitioner.

Now, let's delve into the four-step pranayama exercise:

Find a comfortable seated position with a straight back, and gently close your eyes.

1. Inhale deeply through your nose, taking in the breath as slowly and deeply as possible.
2. Hold your breath for as long as possible until you can't continue.
3. Exhale slowly through the nose as slowly as possible. Emptying your lungs completely.
4. Hold your breath with empty lungs for as long as possible before inhaling again.

Repeat this sequence for approximately five minutes, allowing yourself to fully experience the sensations and effects of the life force within you. This technique is a powerful and effective method to become familiar with the movements of the life force. While the sequence is easy to remember, it is essential to acknowledge that the practice can sometimes feel intense. Moments of feeling overwhelmed or suffocated may arise during the exercise. However, it is crucial to remember that this intensity is the catalyst for quickly boosting the life force, similar to inflating a balloon.

During the practice, you may find yourself experiencing moments of difficulty in breathing or the urge to gasp for air. Yet, looking into the mirror, you may notice a vibrant and alive reflection staring back at you. It is important to remember that nothing harmful happens during the practice; instead, a rejuvenation process occurs within you.

Allow me to share a personal experience to illustrate the transformative power of this practice. Some time ago, after returning home from a long day of work, I caught a glimpse of myself in the mirror and was confronted with an aging face—a tired look with bags under my eyes, visibly displaying the toll of a hectic and stressful life. Being fully immersed in running my window cleaning business, I was constantly stressed and had little time for myself. The damage was evident, and I realized the need for a drastic approach to rejuvenating myself.

I vividly remember venturing into the woods to consciously release everything weighing me down. During that time, I engaged in this pranayama exercise, focusing on deepening my connection with the life force. Upon my return, as I gazed in the mirror again, I was astounded to see that my face had regained its youthful appearance! I rejuvenated myself shortly, erasing approximately seven to eight years of exhaustion and stress! This personal experience truly exemplifies the transformative power of pranayama and the life force.

Furthermore, this pranayama practice can activate a heightened consciousness due to the significant surge in our life force. Often, this practice is accompanied by a trance-like meditation, allowing us to access deeper realms of awareness and insight. While I generally lean towards a more naturalistic form of pranayama, acknowledging that the life force itself is inherently natural, I find the conscious control of our breath somewhat unnatural. However, conscious breathing effectively inhales the life force and enhances our connection.

It is essential to acknowledge that this particular pranayama practice can be incredibly potent, leaving us feeling swiftly recharged and revitalized. Additionally, it is an ideal means to become intimately familiar with the vital life energy within us. Once we are familiar with the sensations and effects of this energy, we can move on to the following method, which feels more organic and natural.

To engage in the next pranayama exercise, also known as PureLife Breath.

1. Breathe slowly through your nose, attentively sensing the life force energy generated at the entrance of your nostrils (where energy centers are). Hold on to this feeling while inhaling.
2. Feel the life force flowing through your nasal passages, filling your lungs and permeating your entire body. While staying connected with this energy, exhale slowly through your nose, releasing the life force from within you.

Repeat this process until you feel fully energized and associated with the life force.

Approach these pranayama experiences with openness and non-judgment, allowing whatever needs processing and release to surface. If at any point you feel discomfort or overwhelmed during the exercises, take a moment to rest and engage in gentle, general breathing before continuing.

Remember to approach these pranayama exercises with curiosity and a willingness to explore and deepen your connection with your inner self. Embrace the journey of breath, and enjoy the transformative and revitalizing effects of tapping into the power of the life force within you.

Chapter 4: Exploration of the Chakras, Kundalini, the Central Channel, and Their Connection to the Life Force

In the previous chapter, we learned how to cultivate the life force through pranayama, or life force breathing. When working with this vital energy, it is essential to have knowledge about the chakra system. Understanding the chakras becomes increasingly critical as we become more familiar with energy flow and how it feels during practices like pranayama. These chakras are energy centers or gateways in the body that generate and perpetuate the life force, also known as energy wheels. This term describes the chakras as rotating wheels or spirals of energy, emphasizing their dynamic nature and role in facilitating energy flow within the body. The concept of these energy centers is ancient and has been described in various cultures. Here are a few examples:

In the context of the Christian book of Revelation, there is mention of the Seven Seals, which are often associated with the seven chakras. Each seal represents a specific spiritual state or phase of consciousness. In esoteric traditions, the chakras are sometimes referred to as seven rays. Each ray has a unique energetic quality corresponding to certain consciousness and spiritual development aspects. The chakras are sometimes depicted as lotus flowers in Hindu and Buddhist traditions. Each chakra is associated with a specific number of lotus petals, carrying symbolic significance. In the Kabbalistic teachings of Judaism, there is mention of energy centers called sefirot. While not directly comparable to the chakras, they share similarities regarding working with subtle energy and spiritual development. These seven chakras, also known as primary chakras, are intricately connected to the body. These energy wheels rotate on life force and transport vital energy to our nerves and organs. Each chakra has its own function that can enhance or diminish the body and mind, depending on how life force energy flows. The chakras are subtle bridges between the physical and metaphysical dimensions, transporting the life force to the nerves, organs, and tissues. Although invisible, they can be perceived through meditation, pranayama, visualization, and life force exercises. As we become familiar with this vital force, observing the possible causes of our physical ailments based on energy becomes more accessible.

Here are the 7 chakras and their effects on our body and mind:

1. Root Chakra: Located at the base of the spine, it influences the adrenal glands, kidneys, pelvic area, and lower digestive system. It regulates metabolism, blood pressure, and the body's response to stress. When balanced, it enhances mental focus and reduces feelings of anxiety and fear.

2. Sacral Chakra: Located two thumb-widths below the navel, it is connected to the reproductive organs, urinary system, and lower intestines. It is associated with water and our ability to adapt to life changes. It influences creativity, emotional stability, self-confidence, happiness, and pleasure. A balanced Sacral Chakra improves libido and creative drive.

3. Solar Plexus Chakra: Located between the navel and the sternum in the upper abdomen, it is associated with

personal power, self-confidence, and self-worth. Balancing and energizing it can bring courage, motivation, and a sense of control over one's life.

4. Heart Chakra: Located in the middle of the chest, it is connected to vital systems such as the heart, lungs, thymus, and circulatory system. It is associated with love, compassion, and empathy, symbolizing the bridge between the physical and spiritual dimensions.

5. Throat Chakra: Located in the throat area, it significantly regulates metabolism and calcium levels, supporting the respiratory and digestive systems. This chakra is closely connected to the thyroid and parathyroid glands. In addition to its physiological functions, the Throat Chakra is associated with communication, creativity, and authenticity. A balanced Throat

Chakra can enhance self-expression, increase understanding of life's purpose, and strengthen intuition. However, a dysfunctional Throat Chakra can cause communication problems and physical throat issues.

6. The third Eye Chakra, also known as the Ajna Chakra, Is located between the eyebrows and is connected to the pituitary and pineal glands. This chakra regulates bodily functions such as the sleep-wake cycle and supports intuition and spiritual understanding. An imbalance in this chakra can lead to headaches, insomnia, and a lack of mental clarity.

7. Crown Chakra: Located at the top of the head, it is essential for regulating bodily functions and maintaining overall health. This chakra is associated with higher consciousness and spiritual connection, leading to increased intuition, inner peace, and a

sense of unity with the universe. By focusing the life force on the Crown Chakra, individuals can cultivate greater self-awareness, compassion, and acceptance while reducing anxiety and depression.

Integrating life force into our daily lives makes us more aware of the chakra system and its functioning. When life force does not flow properly or is blocked, for example, due to inevitable tensions, it adversely affects our body and mind. We can optimize our lives and reap its benefits by cultivating the life force in the body and the chakras.

4.1 The Sub-Chakras

In addition to the primary chakras, I would like to discuss the sub-chakras and their specific role in the body. The sub-chakras are lesser known but can provide additional insights regarding physical ailments. They reside within the primary chakras and regulate the energy flow within each chakra. They can be thought of as smaller wheels within the more giant wheel of the primary chakra, helping to fine-tune the energy that permeates the body.

For instance, the root chakra has four sub-chakras: the coccygeal, perineal, anal, and rectal chakras. The coccygeal chakra is located at the base of the spine and is responsible for grounding and physical stability. The perineal chakra is positioned between the anus and the genitals and is associated with sexual energy. The anal chakra resides in the anus and is responsible for waste elimination from the body. Lastly, the rectal chakra is located in the rectum and is associated with removing toxins from the body.

Moving upward in the body, the sacral chakra has two sub-chakras: the prostatic and ovarian chakras. The prostatic chakra is found in the prostate gland of males and is associated with sexual energy. The ovarian chakra is situated in the ovaries of females and is connected to reproductive power.

The solar plexus chakra comprises three sub-chakras: the gastric, hepatic, and splenic chakras. The gastric chakra resides in the stomach and is linked to the digestive system. The hepatic chakra is located in the liver and is associated with the body's detoxification process. The splenic chakra is in the spleen and connected to the immune system.

Moving up to the heart chakra, we encounter two sub-chakras: the thymic and cardiac chakras. The thymic chakra is in the thymus gland and is associated with the immune system. The cardiac chakra resides in the heart and is connected to emotional balance.

The throat chakra possesses two sub-chakras: the laryngeal and palatine chakras. The laryngeal chakra is located in the larynx and is associated with communication. The palatine chakra resides on the roof of the mouth and is connected to the sense of taste.

Lastly, the third eye chakra encompasses two sub-chakras: the pineal and pituitary chakras. The pineal chakra is located in the pineal gland and is associated with sleep and circadian rhythms. The pituitary chakra is situated in the pituitary gland and is responsible for maintaining hormonal balance.

Understanding the life force and the sub-chakras can assist individuals in identifying and addressing specific imbalances within the primary chakras. Working with the life force and pinpointing particular points like the sub-chakras, individuals can refine the energy flow within their bodies and enhance their overall well-being.

4.2 Additional Chakras

While the seven primary chakras are widely known and discussed, there is a lesser-known realm of various other chakras that deserve our attention. These include the eye, hand, foot, elbow, and knee chakras. Understanding and nurturing these chakras can contribute to a healthier and more prosperous life.

The eye chakras, situated at the center of each eye, play a significant role in visual perception, intuition, and psychic abilities. When these chakras are in balance, they facilitate clear physical and spiritual vision. Imbalances in the eye chakras can lead to eye problems, headaches, and difficulty accessing intuition. For example, the eye's iris serves as a structure that enables sight. It is a circular and thin component located in the center of the eye, regulating the amount of light entering by adjusting pupil size. This protects the retina from excessive light

exposure and contributes to depth
perception, enabling focus on objects at
different distances. When our eye chakras
are blocked, our vision may become blurry.
However, by continuously directing our
attention to the life force within our irises,
we can achieve clarity of vision, similar to
how an eagle sees its prey from afar by
tapping into the life force. In fact, the
physical form of the eyes resembles chakras,
which explains why enhancing them can
improve eyesight. I've had times when my
vision declined temporarily, which can be
frustrating since we always rely on our eyes.
At first, I thought these moments were due
to the early morning hours and the process
of waking up. However, when my vision
stayed blurred, I realized there was more to
it. Considering my parents' vision, with my
mother undergoing laser eye surgery and
my father relying on reading glasses, I
recognized my predisposition to developing
visual impairments. While poor eyesight

often stems from a strained gaze, it can also be associated with avoiding trauma-related experiences. I quickly regained sharper vision by readjusting my eyes through the focus of life force energy in my pupils. I gained a deeper understanding of the intricate workings of the eyes themselves. The eyes bear a physical resemblance to chakras, making it unsurprising that improving these energy centers can enhance our visual capabilities.

Likewise, chakras exist in our hands, enabling us to tap into and transmit life force energy. As a therapist or energy worker, I have had the privilege of assisting many individuals in channeling and facilitating the flow of life force energy in others. The hand chakras in the palms and fingertips are closely associated with our ability to give and receive power and our creative potential. These chakras are essential for healing and energy work, as they facilitate energy flow through touch.

Irregular energy flow in our hand chakras can result in physical issues and difficulties in creativity, motivation, and relationships. We can overcome such challenges with life force by restoring harmony and balance to these chakras, promoting physical well-being, and unlocking our creative capacities.

The foot chakras, situated in the soles of our feet, play a crucial role in grounding and connecting us to the Earth's energy. In addition to regulating balance, stability, and the manifestation of desires in the physical world, these chakras allow us to draw power from the Earth and release any unusable energy.

Below the foot sole, chakras are other chakras that serve as an extension of the body. However, the problem lies in our tendency to identify ourselves solely with the physical body, even though energy extends far below the foot's sole chakras and above our head or crown chakra. The body is simply an aspect of the larger whole. Imbalanced foot chakras can lead to balance issues, difficulties manifesting desires, and feelings of disconnection from the Earth.

Although not commonly discussed, the elbow chakras are intricately connected to the heart chakra and symbolize our ability to fully embrace life. Positioned near the heart center, these chakras promote emotional release and liberation, particularly for individuals struggling to give or receive love. By harmonizing the elbow chakras, we open ourselves to a more profound experience of love and emotional freedom.

Similarly, the knee chakras behind each knee are associated with our ability to move forward. Representing our sense of purpose and our capacity to take action towards our goals, the knee chakras empower us to navigate our chosen path. By nurturing and balancing these chakras, we enhance our sense of purpose, strengthen our determination, and unlock our potential to overcome obstacles and progress in life.

Delving into these other chakras beyond the well-known seven reveals a profound world of energetic potential. The eye, hand, foot, elbow, and knee chakras offer valuable insights into our physical, emotional, and spiritual well-being. By embracing and understanding these chakras, we embark on a transformative journey of self-discovery and empowerment, facilitating a harmonious existence and unlocking the boundless capabilities of our energy systems.

4.3 Kundalini and the Central Channel

Kundalini, rooted in ancient Hindu and yogic traditions, is a powerful and sacred force inherent in us. Originating from the Sanskrit word for "coiled," kundalini is often visualized as a dormant serpent-like energy resting at the base of our spine, within the root chakra. When awakened, it offers immense strength and heightened awareness. As this energy rises along the spine's central channel, traversing the chakras, it catalyzes profound spiritual revelations and transformations in consciousness. The journey of Kundalini awakening is marked by profound physical, emotional, and spiritual metamorphoses.

Kundalini is not a mere abstract concept confined to spiritual traditions; it manifests tangibly in our modern society. It is a mysterious and influential force that permeates every aspect of our lives. We witness its influence in advertisements, stirring our desires; in music videos, evoking deep emotions; in artworks, inspiring our souls; and even in everyday interactions. Kundalini is an inner driving force that propels us to overcome obstacles and tap into our creative potential.

This energetic force is closely intertwined with sexual energy, stemming from the same source of life force and creative power. For specific individuals, the experience of Kundalini energy is tangible, residing dormant within and manifesting as a potent life force. It can give rise to new life and creative expression in various domains. Hence, it is unsurprising that individuals with awakened kundalini often exhibit heightened sexual awareness or remarkable creative abilities.

From my personal perspective as a man, I have observed a strong connection between sexual experiences and the ebb and flow of Kundalini energy. After orgasm, there is often a decline in power, which is understandable as creative energy resides in the testicles and is released during that moment. In tantric practices, the focus is on maintaining sexual energy while avoiding ejaculation, as this cultivation allows Kundalini energy to circulate throughout the body instead of being released. By channeling and conserving sexual energy, the life force or Kundalini energy can be strengthened and directed towards spiritual growth and transformation.

Mastering Kundalini energy is a profound and intricate process that requires awareness of this energy and a willingness to embark on deep self-inquiry. It can lead to extraordinary spiritual experiences and the revelation of higher realms of consciousness.

Kundalini ascends through the spine, navigating the central channel and energizing each chakra. Every chakra possesses distinct characteristics and attributes. The significance of these attributes is directly linked to the chakra where the life force, or Kundalini energy, is most active. For example, if kundalini mainly resides in the second chakra (svadhishthana), sexual energy may be heightened. Tantric philosophy suggests transcending this energy through breathwork, meditation, and asanas, guiding kundalini upward through the central channel, which can lead to profound states of consciousness. If kundalini is primarily present in the heart chakra, feelings of love and compassion may take precedence.

I have pondered whether they are synonymous in contemplating kundalini and life force energy. While each chakra maintains its individuality, they share many similarities. They all share the fundamental life force. Kundalini is distinct but relies on life force energy to progress. Throughout my life, I have experienced numerous intense Kundalini awakenings that induced involuntary convulsive movements, causing me to roll on the ground. Kundalini is akin to electrical energy pulsating through one's being. Focusing on the lower chakras can activate primal instincts like a teenager overwhelmed by hormones. By nurturing and harnessing these instincts, this energy can be transformed into a higher state of being, enabling us to transcend time and space, delving deeper into multidimensional consciousness.

I vividly recall sitting in meditation after an intense lovemaking session and contemplating the possibility of a future relationship with my girlfriend back then. Immediately, I had a vision of her future where she resided in Rotterdam, appearing chaotic as if things were not going well for her. She sat at a table with a unique and distinct wallpaper pattern behind her. Interestingly, I did not see myself in this future, suggesting we would not be together. It was a shocking revelation at that moment. I did not dwell further on this vision and continued embracing the adventure of life.

A few months later, the relationship ended for whatever reasons, and I continued on my path. Two years later, I unexpectedly reencountered my ex-girlfriend in Rotterdam, reigniting the fire of kundalini.

I have noticed throughout my life that sexual compatibility is not guaranteed for everyone. This is related to the strength of Kundalini energy within each individual. Sometimes, individuals aren't compatible but are still drawn to each other due to the kundalini.

After going on a few dates with her, I visited her at her home in Rotterdam, and to my great surprise, I saw the same unique wallpaper in her living room as I had seen in my previous vision two years earlier! I asked her if she had ever sat at that table feeling confused, to which she replied, "Yes, that's true. I did sit there once when things weren't going well for me." How did you know, she asked?

I remember my vision after the sex years earlier when the kundalini moved up the spine.

The concept of visions or multidimensional consciousness could fill an entire book, so I will refrain from delving into it at length.

The human body is not merely a physical entity; it represents a complex network of energy pathways. These pathways act as conduits, carrying and distributing life energy throughout the body, with a central energy channel that runs vertically from the base of our spine to the crown of our head.

The central channel goes by various names, including the "Jacob's ladder" mentioned in the book of Genesis, where Jacob sees a ladder extending from Earth to Heaven with angels ascending and descending upon it. It metaphorically represents the connection between the earthly and divine realms. Gnosis speaks of the "kingdom of heaven" within oneself, accessible through the ascent of kundalini, similar to the biblical story.

This energetic pathway runs vertically along the spine as the main conduit for the flow of life force, or kundalini. The central channel is associated with the awakening and ascension of spiritual energy, leading to higher states of consciousness and spiritual transformation. In Vedic literature, it is known as the "sushumna" or "pranic tube." According to Vedic traditions, activating the central channel is essential for spiritual growth and self-realization. This energy flows through the main channel, bringing balance, healing, and spiritual awakening to the individual. Practices like pranayama and meditation open and purify this energy channel, allowing Kundalini energy to rise, ultimately leading to spiritual enlightenment. The concept of the central channel in Egyptology is called the "djed." The Djed symbolizes stability, endurance, and strength—a representation in ancient Egyptian art resembling a long, straight pillar with crossbars resembling a spine or backbone. It is associated with Osiris, the god of the afterlife, believed to be resurrected with the aid of the Djed. In Egyptian art, the Djed symbolizes the path of spiritual evolution and transformation, representing the body's energetic system, particularly the spinal chakras, crucial in bridging the spiritual and physical realms. Kundalini, or life force, is intimately linked with the Djed, symbolizing the dormant energy residing at the base of the spine. The word "Djed" originates from the Djedi in hermetic teachings, representing spiritual warriors who have mastered their life force energy, capable of utilizing it for healing

and transformative purposes. These Djedi
are revered as protectors of the spiritual
realm, guardians of ancient wisdom, and
holders of profound knowledge.
Interestingly, the Star Wars film series draws
inspiration from these ancient Djedi
principles.

Chapter 5: The Life Force, as in Star Wars and the Vision of Integrated Potential

The Star Wars franchise has transcended the realm of entertainment to become a cultural phenomenon, captivating audiences worldwide with its timeless tale of good versus evil and the power of the force. Central to this epic narrative are the Jedi Knights, revered as the galaxy's guardians of peace and justice. These noble warriors possess extraordinary abilities, tapping into a force that permeates the universe—an energy known as the Life Force.

In the Star Wars universe, the Life Force is portrayed as an interconnecting energy field that binds all living things, shaping their actions and determining their destinies. The Jedi can achieve incredible feats, such as telekinesis, precognition, and mind control, through their training and mastery of the force. However, their teachings emphasize balance and responsibility, urging them to employ their powers only for the greater good.

Remarkably, echoes of this profound concept can be found in ancient Egyptian hermetic teachings, which similarly emphasize the existence of a universal life force. Known as the Djedhi, this eternal energy source is believed to permeate every aspect of creation, from humans and animals to plants and even inanimate objects. It is the lifeblood that sustains the fabric of the universe itself.

The parallels between the Jedi and the Djedhi are striking. Both orders recognize the importance of meditating upon and connecting with the life force to attain higher levels of consciousness and spiritual enlightenment. They understand the interconnectedness of all living things and seek to harness the power of the life force for personal growth and the betterment of society. This philosophy acknowledges the cosmic order and our role within it.

Moreover, both the Jedi and the ancient Egyptians acknowledge the presence of the life force in the physical environment. In the Star Wars universe, the force is said to be present in all matter, permeating rocks, trees, and the natural world. This connection allows Jedi to sense and manipulate their surroundings, utilizing their affinity with the life force. Similarly, the ancient Egyptians believed that the Djedhi infused every aspect of the natural world, emphasizing the importance of respecting and harmonizing with nature.

Furthermore, both the Jedi and the ancient Egyptians recognized the power of symbols and archetypes in representing and harnessing the life force. In Star Wars, the Jedi utilize potent symbols like the lightsaber, the iconic robe, and the emblem of the Jedi Order to represent their dedication to the force and their ideals. Likewise, the ancient Egyptians employed a rich array of images, symbols, and hieroglyphics to convey concepts associated with the Djedhi. These symbols were believed to possess profound mystical significance, capable of elevating consciousness and inspiring spiritual transformation.

The convergence of these themes from Star Wars and ancient Egyptian teachings suggests a more profound, universal truth transcending space and time's boundaries. It implies a shared understanding of the life force and its profound implications for humanity. Whether through the adventures of the Jedi or the wisdom of the Djedhi, these narratives invite us to contemplate our connection to a force greater than ourselves —a force that unites us guides us, and offers the potential for extraordinary transformation.

In conclusion, the relationship between Star Wars, the Jedi, the life force, and ancient Egyptian hermetic teachings is a testament to the enduring power of these concepts throughout history. The parallels between these two systems of thought illuminate our shared human quest for understanding and harnessing the life force that courses through us and the universe. By embracing this universal truth, we can embark on a journey of self-discovery and empowerment, drawing upon the limitless potential of the life force to shape a brighter future for all.

5.1 The Vision of Integrated Potential

We find ourselves standing at the precipice of a profound transformation—a paradigm shift that demands our attention and imagination. In this era of rapid technological advancement, where artificial intelligence looms on the horizon, there is a pressing need to redefine our relationship with technology and rediscover our essence as human beings. While the allure of progress and efficiency may seduce us, we must be cautious not to sacrifice our intrinsic nature in the process. Within this future vision, I see a harmonious integration of technology and humanity, with a renewed emphasis on the social fabric that binds us together. As automation gradually replaces traditional jobs, we are presented with an opportunity to reallocate our time towards introspection, time-out, and exploring the depths of our potential. It is a departure from the old ways, embracing a new paradigm.

Technology, in its many forms, can bring both joy and destruction. It is the wielding of technology that determines its impact on our lives. As we contemplate the possibilities, remember that our bodies and minds are marvels of complexity and advancement, surpassing even the most sophisticated machines. Instead of surrendering ourselves entirely to the allure of technology, we must place our bodies at the forefront of our attention.

Our physical well-being directly influences our overall health and shapes our engagement with the world. While we have made remarkable progress, we have only begun to scratch the surface of our true capabilities. These immense benefits await us by embracing our innate potential without overreliance on technology.

Some may be enticed by merging with artificial intelligence or pursuing trans-humanism as a panacea for human limitations. However, we must explore and harness our inherent potential before seeking external enhancements. Only by nurturing our bodies, harnessing the life force, and truly understanding and caring for them can we find the harmony we seek amidst the advancing tide of technology.

Imagine a future where individuals willingly embrace a symbiotic relationship with technology, utilizing implants or nanodevices to regulate bodily functions, combat diseases, or enhance performance. The possibilities seem awe-inspiring, but we must also consider the potential pitfalls. The power to manipulate our bodies and minds through technology could be abused, leading to a loss of autonomy and unforeseen consequences. It is essential to remember that all forms of technology, no matter how advanced, are derived from nature itself. If we cultivate the life force with the right skills and mindset, we can regulate our bodily functions and tap into our potential, much like the Tibetan yogis.

This notion may seem far-fetched, but consider how quickly we have adapted to new technologies in the past. Learning to ride a bicycle, once a daunting task that took years of practice, has become second nature to most nowadays. Similarly, mastering the inner workings of our bodies and unlocking our dormant life force is a journey that lies within the reach of each of us. Through healthy dieting and practices like yoga, sports, or meditation, we can cultivate balance, awaken our latent potential, and draw upon the wellspring of the life force.

The Star Wars saga, metaphorically portraying the life force, offers a glimpse into the extraordinary feats we can achieve when we tap into our inner power. However, we must adapt this ancient wisdom to the realities of our modern society, marked by rapid technological growth and ever-increasing demands. Embracing practices that honor our bodies, adopting mindful approaches to diet and exercise, and engaging in activities that nurture physical and mental well-being are the pathways that lead us to unlock the life force in our daily lives. Fortunately, many individuals recognize the significance of striking this balance.

In summary, we should recognize our bodies as essential vessels while striving for progress. They are integral to our human experience and deserve our care and attention. As we embark on a journey of self-exploration, let us awaken our untapped potential and embrace the power of the life force within us. By integrating these principles into our lives, we can forge a new facet of modern society that embraces the harmonious interplay between technology and humanity. It is a vision where our bodies and the life force's boundless potential align with our time's

technological advancements, shaping a
future that celebrates the fullness of our
human potential.

Chapter 6: Extraordinary Abilities

Ever since my early years, I have been captivated by the allure of extraordinary abilities. A fascination has persisted throughout my life, driving me to extensively research and explore these exceptional phenomena. I have a clear memory of my ten-year-old self, filled with curiosity and excitement, as I tried to levitate. I imagined the thrill of defying gravity and effortlessly floating in mid-air. Since childhood, I have believed in the possibility of the supernatural, and this pursuit became a prominent focus. This pursuit led me to write this book eventually.

As I grew older, around fifteen, I had my first samadhi—an experience that would profoundly transform me. This encounter was not a conscious pursuit but rather an unexpected outcome of hours spent in deep meditation and my unwavering determination to physically lift my body off the ground.

During that profound meditation, I focused all my intention on levitation, only to encounter a different phenomenon known as samadhi. Derived from Hinduism, samadhi represents a state of profound meditative absorption where the individual self merges harmoniously into the boundless expanse of universal consciousness. It signifies the pinnacle of enlightenment and unity. In that extraordinary encounter, my ego dissolved, blending with the infinite consciousness that permeates all existence. I immersed myself in profound silence, tranquility, and inner peace—a paradoxical realm where I seemed to possess knowledge without consciously knowing anything in total awe-amazement. I was utterly captivated by the splendor of everything around me, with profound torrents of information flooding my awareness.

At that particular time, I was living with my brother and mother, and as is often the case between brothers, a lasting rivalry existed. However, my brother had no clue about my elevated state of being then.

While in that state, my brother intruded upon my bedroom and wanted to attack me without reason, probably because of our rivalry, which had unfolded countless times before. Immersed in his role, he charged toward me, intending to strike. Yet, in that altered state of consciousness, I became an objective observer, devoid of judgment, allowing him to attack, perceiving each movement with crystalline clarity that unfolded in slow motion. I stood there unaffected and motionless, as if the physical realm held no sway over me. Eventually, I effortlessly threw him down the stairs, like removing an insignificant insect as if he were light-feathered. This moment was similar to the iconic scene from The Matrix, where Neo, after being bombarded with a barrage of bullets, miraculously resurrects and effortlessly vanquishes his adversary, Mr. Anderson, embodying a superhuman existence. Once my brother landed somewhere at the bottom of the stairs, I faced a choice—whether to persist in that extraordinary state of being or return to my earthly self. Driven by a small voice within, concerned for my brother's well-being, I opted for the latter. Ultimately, everything unfolded without incident.

Upon reflection, I can now decipher the events that led me to that great state. An extraordinary occurrence unfolded as my energy and focus were on defying gravity and lifting my body. Energy surged forth from within me, transcending the confines of my physical being. In the previous chapter, we explored the concepts of kundalini, chakras, and the sushumna—the central channel. This energy surge coursed through the sushumna, ascended through my crown chakra, also known as Sahasrara, and extended beyond my physical body into the cosmos where other chakras reside. I have often pondered what might have transpired if my brother had never ascended the stairs that day—perhaps it was not my destined time. Following that profound experience, I explored consciousness, encountering numerous instances of samadhi or trance-like states. I reached a period where I let go of all attachments and focused solely on pursuing self-realization. Though I experienced many transcendent moments during this phase, I could not fully grasp and sustain them, as if I was bypassing something crucial. Eventually, I released my pursuit of enlightenment, realizing it would manifest naturally over time.

As a child, my mind was constantly drawn to the allure of extraordinary abilities, contemplating what it would be like to exist for thousands of years in this physical form while gazing at the vastness of space. There is an endless depth to unravel, and I wanted to be a part of it.

Throughout history, tales and legends have captivated our imagination, recounting extraordinary individuals with seemingly superhuman abilities. From Shaolin warriors and qigong masters to yogis, fakirs, and practitioners of spiritual disciplines, these remarkable figures have pushed the boundaries of what we perceive as possible, inviting us to explore the realm of extraordinary human capabilities. In this chapter, we will explore the concept of life force and its intricate connection to these exceptional feats.

While many of us primarily identify with our physical bodies and perceive reality through tangible experiences, delving deeper into the nature of reality, like quantum mechanics and esoteric wisdom, reveals a greater understanding. We realize that physical matter is but a manifestation of energy intricately woven into the vast fabric of the universe. Everything that exists extends beyond our human form. Within this grand tapestry, the life force is pivotal—an empowering and amplifying force that enriches our physical vessel's capacities.

In the qigong practice, masters channel the potent energy of the life force through dedicated training and specific techniques. By cultivating and skillfully directing their life force, these masters transcend the limitations of the physical realm. They showcase the profound influence of the life force, surpassing human comprehension. Astonishingly, they can move objects and even individuals without physical contact, similar to Jedi skills from the iconic Star Wars movie. Such extraordinary manifestations challenge the conventional laws of physics, urging us to reassess our perception of reality and embrace the limitless potential embedded within the life force.

Similarly, the legendary Shaolin warriors have long captivated our collective admiration with their extraordinary physical prowess, attributed to their profound connection with the life force. These indestructible warriors have honed exceptional strength, agility, and resilience through relentless training and unwavering discipline. They can shatter solid objects, withstand powerful impacts, and execute seemingly impossible feats. Their mastery of the life force enables them to transcend the limitations imposed upon the human form, unlocking extraordinary physical abilities that defy the confines of traditional knowledge.

Yogis, too, embark on a profound exploration of the immense potential harbored within the life force through their spiritual practices. By employing techniques such as pranayama—the art of life force breath control—they expand their consciousness and attain profound insights into the vastness of the universe, giving them superhuman abilities. Through intentional channeling and adept guidance of the life force, these yogis can achieve levels of consciousness that grant them deep insights into the universe, rivaling the understanding of renowned astrophysicists without the need for advanced technology, which to most of us is mind-boggling. This deep bond with the life force empowers them to surpass the confines of conventional scientific exploration, achieving a profound comprehension of the cosmos.

Another pathway to unlock our superhuman potential lies in the awakening of kundalini—an innate spiritual energy dormant at the base of the spine. As the kundalini rises, individuals can experience profound spiritual moments and develop heightened psychic abilities. Some people perceive the past, present, and future simultaneously, demonstrating the expanded awareness our life force can unlock.

The examples above only glimpse the wide range of superhuman abilities one can access by delving into the life force. They invite us to question the limitations we impose on ourselves and challenge the conventional understanding of what it means to be human. By recognizing and harnessing the power of the life force, we open ourselves to a transformative journey of self-discovery and empowerment, transcending our perceived boundaries.

In conclusion, tales of superhuman feats are more than just myths or figments of imagination; they echo the vast potential that sleeps within us all. The life force serves as a conduit between the tangible and intangible, ushering us into realms of astounding abilities. While this book primarily emphasizes the healing and rejuvenating facets of life force energy, its implications reach far beyond. As we journey deeper into understanding this energy, we unveil a universe where unparalleled achievements are within reach, pushing the boundaries of our human limitations and inviting us to surpass them.

6.1 Harnessing Life Force via the Palm Chakras

Meditation has always been the guiding light of my journey, an unwavering practice that has shaped my existence almost daily. During a specific period, I devoted ten hours a day to deep and intensive meditation, firmly believing that the way to true awakening resided solely in the stillness of seated practice. Yet, over time, a profound realization dawned upon me—life itself is an eternal meditation, a continuous flow encompassing every facet of our existence. One can discover it in the simplicity of washing dishes, maintaining a focused presence while driving a car, or mindfully engaging in everyday tasks. Meditation transcends the confines of a cushion; it permeates every moment, every action, and every breath. Similar to a Japanese tea ceremony, known as "chanoyu" or "sado," with its grace and artistry, it can become a spiritual and meditative experience, inviting us to cherish and connect with the essence of the present moment.

Among the vivid memories of my journey, one incident stands out—a moment of cleansing windows in the bitter embrace of freezing temperatures below subzero. As nearby skaters glided gracefully over icy

surfaces, I immersed my hand in the frozen
water to clean the windows. I climbed an
aluminum ladder blanketed in a glistening
shroud of snow on a slippery surface. The
water soaked my clothes, transforming
them into icy garments adorned with
delicate icicles. Such was the nature of my
work as a self-employed entrepreneur in
winter time with little time off, no sick
leave, and the demand to clean not just one
house but an average of 20 to 30 homes per
day. Snow and frozen windows seemed
impossible obstacles, threatening to freeze
my physical body and spirit. Confronted
with this daunting challenge, I felt
compelled to forge my path. I realized that
coldness corresponds to a lower frequency
as the temperature drops. Drawing from the
wisdom of Tibetan yogis who defy the
elements through their profound control, I
discovered I could withstand the harsh cold
by slowing down my movement and
activating my life force. Even at minus

seven degrees, as my hands touched snowballs and icicles, an astonishing absence of coldness enveloped me—a peculiar sensation that defied conventional logic. I learned to endure the harshest conditions by correctly utilizing the life force. Remarkably, what was once a burdensome task transformed into an experience of joy and wonder? Liberated from the clutches of suffering, I reveled in the delicate touch of melting snowflakes on my face. Amidst winter's chill, I found myself transported to a realm of enchantment, where the landscape donned the guise of a whimsical fairy tale.

But before this revelation, the path leading to that moment was fraught with hardship. I departed from the confines of formal education at a tender age, opting for independent work. At seventeen, I established my window-cleaning business, demanding persistence and resourcefulness. Despite engaging in various jobs, I grappled with authority, finding it burdensome to meet its demands. Given the circumstances, window cleaning appeared suitable, offering both autonomy and flexibility. However, beneath the surface, a profound interest in spirituality simmered within me, beckoning me toward introspection and a quest for answers that transcended the superficial realms of external representation. My mantra crystallized: "You don't have to go to India to seek a guru; instead, discover the guru within the tapestry of existence, where life emerges as the greatest teacher."

The challenges were especially relentless in the winter months, particularly during the early stages of my window cleaning career. To counter the biting cold, I resorted to a seemingly harmless practice—I filled my bucket with boiling water to provide comfort and warmth to my frozen hands. Little did I realize that this well-intentioned remedy would eventually exact a toll on my physical well-being. The sharp contrast between the searing heat of the water and the frosty ambiance, mere degrees below freezing, gradually made my hands vulnerable. The very act of shaking someone's hand could produce audible cracks, even on the hottest of summer days. Furthermore, my knees had tension that manifested as an apparent noise of cracking sounds whenever I settled into a seated position or attempted a squat. The manifestations of this wear and tear were impossible to ignore.

Fortunately, the tide began to turn through the awakening of my knee and palm chakras. By activating the life force within these focal points, I discovered a newfound liberation from the restraints of discomfort. Miraculously, much of the continuous cracking dissipated into my memory within a few days. This transformative experience underscored the power and potential of the life force.

Now, let's delve into harnessing this energy via our palm chakras.

1. Find a serene and comfortable place to either sit or stand.
2. Position your hands approximately 5 to 10 centimeters apart, with palms facing each other.
3. Familiarize yourself with the optimal distance between your hands, allowing for a naturally comfortable position.
4. Once settled, please direct your attention to the palms of your hands, gently resting your awareness upon them. You may experiment by rotating your hands subtly, creating an energetic connection between them.
5. As time passes, you will perceive the energy flowing between your palms. This ethereal current may reveal itself as tingling sensations, a magnetic

field-like presence, warmth, or even a subtle yet discernible pressure. Proceed to the next step when you feel attuned and at ease with this energy flow, this manifestation of life force.

6. Remove one hand from the equation, focusing solely on the remaining hand. Please direct your attention toward feeling the energy flowing through that solitary hand, free from the support of its counterpart. As you embrace this stage of the practice, guide the power of the life force toward your wrist.

7. Can you also perceive this energy in other parts of your body? With a relaxed and receptive body, concentrate on this vibrant energy, keenly observing any sensations that arise. After a while, can you amplify the life force in areas where you feel its presence? Notice the delicate tingling sensations akin to the gentle

prickling of innumerable needles or a
surge of warmth that permeates your
being. Allow this natural process to
unfold, maintaining a state of
attentive and objective observation.
Observe the inherent movements of
the vibrancy within you, for within
this observation lies the key to
activating and preserving the life
force.

8. Can you increase the strength of this
   energy? If you initially felt it as two
   units of force, can you raise it to three,
   four, or even eight units? Please focus
   on the energy flow, building its
   sensation through gentle yet
   intentional pressure, and keep
   concentrating.

9. Finally, can you allow this energy to
   traverse your entire being, surging
   through the channels of your body
   without hindrance? Surrender to this
   process, fully immersing yourself in

the profound experience of the life force's dance within you. Feel free to explore the effects of nurturing and strengthening the life force's presence.

Approach this exercise with an open mind, a spirit of curiosity, and a willingness to learn. Through unwavering dedication and consistent effort, you will witness mastery unfolding in utilizing the life force energy that courses through your being. By activating this potent energy, your body initiates its innate self-healing mechanisms, tapping into a realm of profound restoration and balance. It is crucial to acknowledge that the life force encompasses a higher consciousness, surpassing the limitations of our conscious selves. This higher consciousness knows precisely where it needs to go, what areas require healing, and how to restore equilibrium within the body. By embracing this highly effective method, you will witness the healing of fractures, the regeneration of cartilage, and the newfound strength and vitality of weak muscles.

During your sessions, sensations may arise, which some might perceive as pain. Yet, this pain is distinct—it transcends conventional discomfort and manifests as a presence—a discernible embodiment of the life force's transcendence. Paradoxically, pain becomes an indicator, a signpost directing your attention toward activating the life force within your body. I have incorporated this profound method into one of my training programs, witnessing its transformative impact firsthand. The simplicity of this practice is a testament to its potency. I wholeheartedly encourage the discovery of joy in self-empowerment and the abundant rewards accompanying such a revelation. It is upon these timeless principles that these teachings find their foundation, resonating with seekers of truth and illuminating the path to self-realization.

133

As you embrace the cultivation of life force through your palm chakras, remember that you hold the infinite wellspring of energy and potential within you. Understand that the life force is all around. May this practice serve as a gateway to unlocking your innermost power, allowing you to embrace the fullness of your being and manifest profound transformation in your life's tapestry.

6.2 The Life Force Body

In my quest for extraordinary potential and a deep understanding of the life force, I have discovered a revelation that can revolutionize our existence. It is the recognition that we can unleash the flow of life force energy, allowing it to course through our bodies entirely and revitalize us on every level. Like powerful batteries, our bodies can charge fully and infuse us with abundant vitality and boundless potential. Conversely, when our energy levels decline to a mere 15 percent, we resemble those struck by the debilitating flu, barely able to muster the strength to move. This undeniable truth highlights the fundamental role of energy in our lives, no matter the challenges we face or the endeavors we pursue.

Especially in those demanding moments when the weight of the world seems to rest upon our shoulders—navigating daily responsibilities, pursuing ambitious goals, nurturing our children, conquering mundane tasks, persevering through trials, immersing ourselves in enriching activities like treks and sports, and even during moments of rest and self-renewal—we desperately need an inexhaustible energy supply. Imagine a reality where our life forces effortlessly and continuously hums in the background, regardless of our actions. Can you envision the transformative impact this would have on our lives? Once we intimately understand the essence of life force energy and master the art of perpetual motion, channeling its power becomes second nature—a seamless accomplishment. We can summon its vital energy even while engaging in everyday activities—conversing, maneuvering through traffic, waiting at a traffic light, or pushing our physical limits during exercise. Life force energy becomes an extension of ourselves, an omnipresent force that enhances every aspect of our lives.

The Life Force Body, also known as the energetic, subtle, or pranic body, is an integral part of our being, intricately interwoven with our physical form. Picture this remarkable phenomenon as a radiant, luminous field that envelops us. Within this ethereal tapestry, a network of channels, centers, and vortices facilitates the unrestricted flow of vital energy, ensuring our overall well-being is supported. It is akin to a majestic river coursing through its banks, nurturing all living beings in its wake. The life force surges within us, revitalizing every cell, organ, and fiber of our being, breathing life into our existence.

While practices like activating the chakras in the palms of our hands contribute to cultivating life force energy, the realm of the Life Force Body offers an expansive panorama for its activation. Directing our intention throughout our entire being, like the extension of our hand palm chakras, we tap into the extraordinary power contained within the life force.

Just as a river curves through diverse landscapes, nourishing all living beings in its wake, life force energy permeates every aspect of our existence. It breathes life into our cells, fuels our thoughts and emotions, and guides us spiritually. Likewise, the Life Force Body encompasses us wholly, supporting us through life's trials and tribulations and elevating us with a profound sense of divine connection. This interconnectedness is the essence of the Life Force Body.

The activation of the Life Force Body signifies the awakening of a vibrant energy field that extends beyond the boundaries of our physical form. This energetic conduit facilitates the free-flowing current of vital energy, nurturing and revitalizing every facet of our being, from the core of our physical body and vital organs to the intricate matrix of our tissues and cells. When activated, it permeates our skin and energy centers, infusing them with life-giving energy along the meridians that crisscross our human vessels.

Like the etheric body, the Life Force Body is a conduit that seamlessly bridges our awareness between the physical and metaphysical planes. By embracing a deeper understanding of the Life Force Body, we transcend the confines of conventional physical laws, unraveling the mysteries of our biological nature. Throughout the preceding chapters, we have gained clarity and insight into the life force through transformative practices such as pranayama, the central channel, and activating the chakras in our palms. Now, with the Life Force Body as our guide, we transcend these practices, expanding our horizons and stepping into a realm where intention, continuity, and the rhythmic flow of the life force converge. The key lies in engaging with the vast Life Force Body, reaching beyond the physical realm by relaxing and channeling the energy from the ether into our being for extended periods. Through this profound connection, we tap into the full spectrum of its immense potential, unleashing the boundless power that resides within.

In our normal state, we often fixate solely on our physical or mental conditions, ignoring the deeper realms of our being. Many individuals are so immersed in their rational minds that they fail to connect with their bodies, perceiving only their heads, neck, and shoulders. However, by consciously attuning to our sensory experiences, we shift away from the mind's constant chatter. Sensation becomes a counterbalance to thought—a gateway to a more embodied existence.

As we direct our attention to the various sensations within us—whether they manifest as pain, itchiness, cramps, or tension—we awaken a heightened awareness of our physicality. Gradually, we disengage from the continuous stream of thoughts dominating our consciousness. Yet, it is crucial to recognize that while our physical bodies serve as the foundation of our existence within the physical realm, they are subject to imperfections and vulnerabilities, such as illness and the effects of aging. Our physical reality, though tangible, can be seen as an abstract representation of a more fundamental truth: ENERGY.

Let us consider the Life Force Body as our primary essence, with the physical body as a secondary role. If we embrace this perspective, we find ourselves living in a fascinating inversion—an inversion that invites introspection and contemplation. Countless debates and speculations exist regarding the relationship between consciousness and the body. Does consciousness reside within the body, or does the body exist within the expansive domain of consciousness? The answer to this inquiry is not straightforward, for, as you may already know, my experiences often transcend conventional boundaries, embracing a multidimensional perspective that extends to every facet of life, including physical embodiment. In this expansive view, the body manifests within the vast expanse of consciousness.

Consciousness, when defined, transcends the limitations of individualized perception. It encompasses the entirety of creation—a magnificent tapestry interwoven with the fabric of existence. From a holistic perspective, we may observe that diseases often originate in the mental body, like seeds that sprout and subsequently infiltrate the emotional body. Eventually, these disturbances may manifest as ailments in the physical body. Thus, the interconnectedness of our being becomes evident—the Life Force Body, an extension of consciousness, nourishes and influences all aspects within us.

Our awareness shifts as we embark on a journey of deepening familiarity with the Life Force Body and truly attune ourselves to its subtle currents. We begin to transcend the physical body's limitations, embracing the full potential and vitality offered by the Life Force Body.

A vivid memory comes to mind. While washing windows, my ladder suddenly slipped from under my feet. At that moment, I thought about the Life Force Body, which, fortunately, was also active while I was working. My ladder slipped due to the icy conditions caused by freezing rain that day. I fell from a height of 5 meters. Although I experienced somewhat pain, fortunately, I could continue working. If my Life Force Body had not been active, I would have likely broken something. Just seconds before my ladder gave way, I contemplated Shaolin warriors and their ability to endure heavy blows with their bodies. The activation of the Life Force Body immediately manifested the answer.

Exercise:

1. Adopt a comfortable position and relax your body.
2. Feel the life force energy flowing through your body. Notice how your body responds to it. If you need help feeling the life force, refer to the earlier exercises in this book.
3. Like cultivating your life force energy through the palm chakras, you can also absorb energy through your skin and nourish your entire body with vital energy. Visualize an energy field around you, extending about a few centimeters beyond your body, and focus your intention on it.
4. Allow the energy to flow inward gradually until it fills your entire body.
5. Maintain a connection with this energetic form or body as you detach

or release from your physical body. In other words, you're making a paradigm shift in consciousness. Remember to keep your body relaxed while building the energy or life force as you do this.

Once filled with this energy, you can let life force flow through your chakras, such as your crown and root chakras. These two points can act as positive and negative terminals like a battery.

This transformation covers the way to a life of prosperity, not only in the material sense but also in terms of spiritual and holistic well-being. By nurturing our connection with the Life Force Body, we embark on a transformative path that reveals the untapped reservoirs of energy residing within us, propelling us toward a deep integration of mind, body, and spirit. This integration unlocks the gateway to a life of limitless possibilities and profound fulfillment.

6.3 Harnessing the Power of the Life Force in Everyday Life

As we have noticed, the life force is not limited to spiritual warriors like The Jedi or individuals pursuing esoteric practices. It is a force anyone can harness and utilize, especially in modern society.

It doesn't matter if you're a doctor, lawyer, athlete, housewife, or teacher. The life force is available to anyone open to it.

By familiarizing ourselves with the sensation of the life force and consciously activating it, we can incorporate its energy into our everyday activities, infusing it with vitality and intention.

In the past, people have traditionally identified physical exercises as a means to activate the life force. Whether through strict workouts at the gym, yoga sessions, or martial arts practice, these activities tap into the reservoir of energy within us, revitalizing our bodies and minds. However, the integration of the life force goes far beyond these conventional methods because we go straight to the core of our being and the life force itself. Like the Life Force Body, we can integrate it into everyday tasks, such as writing, conversing, waiting, watching movies, walking, engaging in physically demanding work, and even adding them to our workouts. By bringing awareness to the life force and consciously directing its flow, we elevate the quality of these activities. The life force is a supportive technology that enhances our overall well-being, making every moment of our lives more vibrant and purposeful. We can even take it further by adding a healthy diet and regular fasting to our routine. Depending on the person and preferences.

Although engaging with life force energy daily is advisable, it is not obligatory. I have periods when I am less focused on it, especially when things are going well for me. It depends on my preference at that moment. It is also beneficial to recognize the difference between daily practice, occasional engagement, and not engaging with the life force. If I ignore life force energy entirely, it will eventually affect my health or age. So, I will continue to use methods like the Life Force Body for the rest of my life. I aim to remain youthful and have time to continue developing myself. I find life too beautiful to let it pass me by, especially lacking energy.

I cannot spend the rest of my life passively sitting in front of the television when I can actively participate in creating my own storyline. I've noticed that most people only start living around their fifties, but their bodies begin to deteriorate by then. Their mindset no longer aligns with their physical condition. How often have I heard people say, "If only I were 20 again with the knowledge I have now? I would have done many things differently." Everyone makes mistakes; it's part of life. We all regret certain things, but we also learn from our mistakes. That's what shapes who we are. What if our bodies cooperate with our mindsets, even in the later stages of life? Then it doesn't matter how old we are. Age is just a label. We are not our age; we are infinite consciousness having a human experience.

I've realized it took me a long time to reach where I am now. My life is only beginning or entering a new level, and I will continue to do so. For example, I still want to learn skateboarding, something I still need to make time for. Time is relative, especially when harnessing the life force.

If you enjoy many things as I do, sometimes you have to be selective and prioritize. Fortunately, I've always been able to cultivate and apply this potent energy to my life, which allows me to transcend time.

This way, even later in my life, I can do the things I have always wanted to do. For example, I would love to lock myself up, work in a music studio, and create for the love of music. I also want to have my own art studio, participate in exhibitions, and design clothing. Additionally, I would like to take flying lessons and engage in particular sports. These are just a few examples. Although they may not be at the top of my bucket list, they still seem enjoyable.

Don't be mistaken. So far, I have been able to do so much in this life. I have lived multiple lives within this one. Someone once said, "You die multiple times in one life," I agree.

The intended meaning is not the physical death but rather the act of shedding old beliefs, identities, or persistent aspects of oneself that no longer serve a purpose. It is also known as the "Dark Night of the Soul." This reminds me of Kali.

Hindus revere Kali as an essential goddess who embodies destruction and transformation. Artistic representations frequently depict her as a fearsome, dark goddess with four arms, a protruding tongue, and a necklace of severed heads adorning her neck. Her appearance can be intimidating, but her essence and spiritual meaning are deeper.

The name "Kali" is derived from the Sanskrit word "kala," which means "time." Kali is associated with eternal time and symbolizes life's inevitable changes and cycles. She represents the death of the ego and the transient, making space for new growth and rebirth.

In that sense, Kali embodies the maternal force that renews and transforms the universe, emphasizing the importance of integrating this energy, similar to the infinite and ever-flowing life force energy, where forms constantly arise and dissipate. This also goes for our cells and bodies.

We should keep this as a reminder that we shouldn't hold on to the life force but rather move along with it. The integration of the life force into our routines offers numerous benefits. We experience improved endurance, heightened energy levels, accelerated injury recovery, enhanced mood, and increased tolerance for the challenges that come our way. Instead of relying solely on external factors to sustain us, we learn the art of self-management through inner engineering. This concept, often emphasized by spiritual teacher Sadhguru, refers to harnessing our internal resources and abilities to navigate and enhance our being. While external resources can help improve our lives' quality. External resources are often limited, especially in third-world countries.

External resources, such as specific medical treatments, are often limited because they can be costly. Only some people are privileged enough to undergo such treatments. I am a utopian and believe that medical treatments should be free. The fact that there is still so much poverty and illness is disgraceful. We have failed as a society, where a football player earns millions and a garbage collector earns a minimum wage. We as a society need drastic changes. Still, "All changes begin with oneself." The change applies to harnessing the life force that is always available, just like the energy from the sun, which is free. By consciously engaging with the life force, we access a wellspring of vitality that aids in restoring and optimizing our holistic being.

Furthermore, the integration of the life force into our daily routines can yield a myriad of benefits. By cultivating a symbiotic relationship with this potent force, we can enhance our endurance, amplify our energy levels, expedite recovery from injuries, uplift our moods, and augment our tolerance for life's challenges. Rather than relying solely on external influences or circumstances, we embark on a self-management journey through the profound art of inner engineering. As we familiarize ourselves with the presence of the life force and conscientiously activate it during various activities, we unlock the door to profound personal transformation. Through this process, our mental capabilities become sharpened, our emotional well-being deepens, and our physical prowess flourishes.

Integrating the life force into our daily lives is a gateway to holistic self-improvement. As we refine our sensitivity to the life force

and nurture its presence in all we do, we
become architects of our well-being,
witnessing firsthand the harmonious fusion
of mind, body, and spirit. By embracing the
interconnectedness of our inner and outer
worlds, we embark on a remarkable journey
of self-discovery and empowerment.

Chapter 7: Life Force, Pain, and the Power of Releasing Tension within the Body

As I delved into the depths of my meditative practice, a remarkable revelation unfolded: pain, that mysterious and intricate human experience, is intimately intertwined with the boundless currents of life force energy. However, as my understanding deepened, I realized that pain's true essence defies the conventional concept of pain. Instead, it indicates the vibrant life force energy actively pulsating within the areas that evoke discomfort—a transparent sign of vitality and the potential for profound transformation.

I have always worked extremely hard and pushed myself to the limit. I went at it like a machine, whether it was laying streets, working in construction, or washing windows. I seemed to have endless energy. It was only possible thanks to my tremendous life force. I still remember times when I slept only four hours a day, then worked like a machine from around 6:00 a.m. until 5:00 p.m., and sometimes even longer, only to party again the following evening. I could feel the pain in my body as I sat against the wall, but it served as a mere signal indicating the direction of my attention and life force. It no longer felt like ordinary pain but rather like a healing pain, which didn't feel discomfort. It allowed me to maintain my lifestyle and get the most out of my physical condition. Athletes would significantly improve their performance if they cultivated their life forces to prevent injuries and discomfort. The life force enables us to recover fast.

This invites us to explore, urging us to navigate the intricate relationship between pain and the life force energy that flows through our very being. By activating and nurturing the life force, we open ourselves to a great perspective that offers fresh insights and illuminates pathways to alleviate suffering and embark on a transformative healing journey. Throughout this chapter, we will venture into the labyrinthine connection between pain and the life force, unraveling its enigmas and gaining invaluable insights into managing and metamorphosing our existence marred by pain.

Pain undoubtedly encompasses a multifaceted phenomenon surrounding sensory and emotional dimensions. Various sources contribute to its origins, ranging from physical injuries and illnesses to the profound depths of emotional turmoil. Yet, we must transcend the limited perception of pain as mere discomfort and suffering.

When this vital energy flows harmoniously, its currents guide us toward radiant health and a comprehensive equilibrium. Nevertheless, when imbalances or blockages interrupt its smooth flow, pain and various discomforting symptoms arise as unsettling messages from the vital life force, signaling that our energy flow is hindered or disrupted within the intricate framework of our physical and energetic existence but doesn't worry the life force is changing it positively.

Activating and nurturing life force energy is a potent tool in our quest to address pain and facilitate profound healing. By directing our unwavering focus toward the area of discomfort, we ignite a powerful surge of life force energy, channeling it to that specific region and infusing it with renewed vitality. Its intensified flow catalyzes unblocking obstructions, releasing stagnant energies, and orchestrating restoring harmonious balance within our being.

Moreover, we realize that pain, standing at the threshold of the life force itself, unveils a gateway to access the methods and practices we have acquired, enabling us to forge an intimate connection and harness the transformative power that lies within.

At the core of our effort lies the transformation of our perspective on pain—a paradigm shift that unfolds as we engage with the life force energy. Instead of perceiving pain as an adversary to be avoided or suppressed, we approach it with unwavering compassion. Pain, when illuminated by this newfound light, metamorphoses into a profound vessel of communication from our physical form. It becomes an inner compass that guides us toward areas that demand deep attention and nurturing care. Embracing pain with openness and acceptance, we deeply explore its underlying messages, utilizing the life force energy as a remarkable catalyst to transform our relationship with pain.

This transformative journey involves cultivating heightened awareness, unwavering acceptance, and unbeatable resilience in facing pain's challenges.

In essence, comprehending the intricate interplay between pain and the life force energy weaves a tapestry of wisdom, endowing us with a novel and enlightened approach to pain management. By activating and nurturing the life force within us, we unlock the gates to enhance energy flow, alleviate obstructions that impede our vitality, and undergo a profound metamorphosis in our perception of pain. As we dedicate ourselves to devoted practice and delve into the deep depths of our existence, we embark upon a sacred voyage, harnessing the inherent power of the life force to foster profound healing, holistic well-being, and the attainment of a harmonious existence that transcends the boundaries of suffering.

7.1 The Power of Releasing Tension within the Body

Humans are creatures of habit, finding comfort in familiar routines and patterns. However, even when these patterns do not serve us, we tend to cling to them. This attachment extends to the practices within ourselves, leading to a profound impact on our well-being. This phenomenon is closely tied to our need for existential security, as venturing into the unknown can be daunting. When faced with the unfamiliar, alarm bells ring within us, causing us to close ourselves off, hold on tightly, or suppress our emotions. Consequently, tension arises due to these habits of holding on, avoiding the unknown, or hiding our true selves. Unfortunately, these habits can have harmful long-term effects on our physical bodies.

This tension can be observed in our relationships with others, such as toxic partnerships where individuals choose to remain together despite their awareness of their incompatibility. Ending such a relationship may mean facing solitude or encountering an even worse situation. Thus, they remain trapped in harmful patterns because they fear the unknown. We also witness this behavior in individuals imprisoned for extended periods, as they may resist leaving their familiar reality, fearing the uncertainty beyond. These habits can also manifest internally in poor posture or a permanently tense body. We may not even realize that our organs are not functioning optimally due to the tension we have grown accustomed to. This tension becomes our accepted norm, and we are oblivious to the possibility of a better, more accessible existence within ourselves.

In contemplating this, I am reminded of the principles of Bhakti yoga, a spiritual practice originating from ancient Indian traditions and yogic philosophy. Bhakti, meaning "devotion" in Sanskrit, embodies the essence of surrender and love. Unlike other forms of yoga that focus primarily on physical postures and breathing exercises, Bhakti yoga revolves around cultivating an inner attitude of devotion and surrender. It involves opening our hearts and approaching everything in life with compassion. By embracing these principles, we can dissolve the blockages, patterns, and tensions within ourselves.

In previous chapters, we delved into the primary causes of aging and disease, identifying stress as a leading factor. Stress gives rise to tension fields within our bodies, obstructing the natural flow of energy. Over time, we become accustomed to these tension fields, perceiving them as usual. Our sense of identity also plays a crucial role in perpetuating these patterns as we hold onto familiar habits.

While a certain degree of tension is to be expected, ranging from the "standard" to the harmful, understanding the impact of these tension fields on our life force is essential. Tension fields disrupt the flow of life force energy within specific areas of our bodies. Excessive tension hinders the proper circulation of this vital energy, making it challenging for our bodies to heal. Thus, relaxing and generating life force energy is crucial to our well-being.

Often, we may be unaware of the tensions present within our bodies. Prolonged sitting in unnatural positions or assuming specific postures required by our jobs can contribute to these tensions. Yoga is a valuable tool to help us restore a more natural stance and alleviate these tensions. We can strengthen our muscles, increase flexibility, and promote proper body alignment by practicing specific yoga poses, known as asanas. This corrective approach enables us to address imbalances and release the accumulated tension.

In addition to traditional yoga poses, incorporating complementary elements such as the Life Force Body can maximize the benefits of our yoga routine, making it easier to perform. Getting a massage or other forms of relaxation optimizes the life force within the body. Nonetheless, it is crucial to remain conscious of the tensions within our bodies, as they can obstruct the flow of life force energy.

In my lifelong exploration of life force energy through direct experience, I have observed that intense tension fields can significantly interfere with healing. We also see this with the natural facelifting method later described in this book. Even when we believe ourselves to be relaxed, underlying tensions may persist, particularly about specific complaints or illnesses. Introspection may be necessary to uncover and address these tensions. Relaxing the body while cultivating life force energy cannot be overstated—it is essential.

In conclusion, we often find comfort in familiar patterns, even when they do not serve us. This attachment to the known creates tensions and blocks within our bodies, relationships, and overall well-being. With its emphasis on devotion and surrender, Bhakti yoga offers a transformative path to dissolve these patterns and cultivate love and compassion within ourselves. We can release tension and find greater harmony by opening our hearts and embracing the unknown.

The impact of tension on our bodies and life force energy is profound. Stress and habitual tension fields disrupt the natural flow of life force energy, hindering our body's natural ability to heal and repair itself. Incorporating yoga, particularly asanas, into our lives can restore a natural posture, strengthen our muscles, and release tension. Adding the Life Force Body to our practices, such as yoga, can enhance our performance drastically.

It is vital to be aware of the tensions within our bodies and actively relax while cultivating life force energy. By acknowledging and addressing these tensions, we can promote healing, prevent further harm, and embark on a path of self-discovery through gnosis or direct experience.

As we journey towards holistic well-being, let us embrace the wisdom of Bhakti yoga. We can find profound healing and fulfillment by releasing patterns, nurturing devotion, and cultivating a harmonious relationship with ourselves and the world around us.

Chapter 8: The Sacred Heart, thymus gland, and the life force

While exploring life force energy through direct experience, I made a fascinating discovery that immediately captured my attention. Whenever I activated my Life Force Body and felt the urge to yawn, something extraordinary occurred near the sternum around the thymus gland, also known as the sacred heart. From this point, I experienced a sensation akin to liquid metal rushing through my body.

As I delved deeper into this phenomenon, I realized that focusing on the sacred heart or thymus gland unleashed a surge of energy that amplified the life force. Astonishingly, this resulted in instantaneous healing and the distinct sensation of flowing liquid metal or taste. I conducted numerous experiments, leading me to conclude that the thymus gland releases stem cells, which give an added sense that contributes to the strengthening of the body.

This discovery holds immense promise for further exploration and understanding of the intricate connection between life force energy and the thymus gland. We could gain valuable insights into these phenomena' potential healing and regenerative powers through continued research and experimentation.

The Sacred Heart's profound symbolism can be traced back to ancient civilizations. Although its specific depiction and interpretations may have varied across cultures, the concept of the sacred heart as a representation of a mystical and divine essence has remained prominent throughout history. For instance, the heart was significant in ancient Egypt and considered the seat of wisdom, intelligence, and emotions. It played a crucial role in the afterlife, where it was weighed against the feather of Ma'at, the goddess of truth and justice, to determine the worthiness of the deceased to enter the eternal realm.

Similarly, in ancient Mesopotamia, the heart was associated with intelligence, emotions, and intuition, believed to be the dwelling place of the gods within an individual. Rituals and offerings were performed to appease the gods residing in the heart, seeking their guidance and protection.

In ancient Greece, the heart was revered as the soul's dwelling place, a source of love, wisdom, and spiritual insight. Philosophers like Pythagoras and Empedocles attributed significant importance to the heart as the center of perception, understanding, and connection to the divine.

In ancient India, the heart was described as the abode of the divine in the Upanishads, sacred texts that emphasized the convergence of the individual self (Atman) and the universal self (Brahman) within the heart. It was associated with spiritual illumination and realizing one's true nature.

Pre-Columbian Mesoamerican civilizations, such as the Aztecs and Maya, held the heart in great spiritual esteem. Human sacrifice was performed to nourish the gods and maintain cosmic order, believing that removing the heart from sacrificial victims released their divine essence and appeased the deities.

While these ancient cultures may not have depicted the Sacred Heart precisely as it is commonly understood today, the belief in the heart as a sacred and vital entity resonates throughout their beliefs and practices. The heart's association with wisdom, spirituality, and connection to the divine remains consistent, highlighting its enduring significance as a symbol of sacredness in human spirituality.

When examined through the lens of Hermetic and Gnostic principles, the Sacred Heart reveals profound symbolism and mystical significance. It embodies the essence of divine love, spiritual transformation, and esoteric knowledge, making it a potent symbol deserving of exploration.

In Hermetic philosophy, the Sacred Heart embodies the divine, manifesting the purest form of love and compassion. It symbolizes the heart of God, a holy flame that burns within every human being. One can tap into an unlimited source of love and wisdom by connecting with the Sacred Heart.

From a Gnostic perspective, the Sacred Heart transcends the physical realm as a gateway to higher spiritual realities. It symbolizes the union of divine feminine (Sophia) and divine masculine (Christ), resulting in a spiritual alchemy that leads to self-realization and enlightenment.

The thorns surrounding the Sacred Heart depict the trials and challenges encountered on the spiritual path. They represent the obstacles, illusions, and egoic attachments one must overcome to access the divine realms. Furthermore, these thorns symbolize the transformative power of suffering as they wound and purify the heart, refining one's spiritual essence.

Devotion to the Sacred Heart involves cultivating a deep connection with the divine through contemplation, prayer, and meditation. By turning inward and connecting with the divine flame, individuals can experience a profound union with the divine and awaken higher consciousness. This inner journey leads to the realization that the Sacred Heart is not merely a symbol but a living reality within the depths of one's being.

The Sacred Heart also serves as a guide on the path of self-discovery and spiritual evolution. It teaches individuals to embody compassion, forgiveness, and unconditional love for others and themselves. By embracing the qualities of the Sacred Heart, individuals become conduits of divine grace, radiating love and compassion into the world.

In Hermetic and Gnostic teachings, the Sacred Heart represents the eternal flame of love and wisdom within every soul, akin to a divine blueprint. It invites individuals to embark on an inner journey of self-discovery, leading to a profound communion with the holy and realizing their true nature. Through the sacred alchemy of the heart, individuals can embrace their godly heritage and awaken to the infinite possibilities within them. The story of Jesus performing miracles comes from this divine flame or life force produced within this sacred area.

During the early stages of embryonic development, the heart and lungs emerge as among the first organs. This underscores the vital role of the heart in sustaining life, arguably surpassing that of the brain.

Embryogenesis reveals the heart's transformation from a primitive structure into a complex organ that pumps oxygenated blood. Serving as the central hub of the circulatory system, the heart ensures the delivery of vital nutrients and oxygen to every cell, tissue, and organ in the body.

The heart's early formation before the brain highlights its fundamental importance in supporting the growth and development of other organs. Its rhythmic contractions and blood circulation give the developing brain the necessary oxygen and nutrients to thrive.

While the brain is responsible for higher cognitive functions, consciousness, and complex thought processes, the heart's primary function of pumping oxygenated blood is indispensable. Without a functioning heart, the brain would be deprived of oxygen and nutrients, impairing its growth and overall functionality.

It is crucial to note that the brain's vital role should be noticed, as it governs our perception, learning, and decision-making capabilities. However, the heart's role in pumping oxygenated blood is essential for ensuring the brain's survival and proper functioning.

The thymus gland, often called the master gland of immunity, holds immense significance despite its small size. Situated in the upper chest behind the sternum, the thymus plays a crucial role in our overall well-being and the flow of life force energy. The functions of the thymus gland and its profound connection to life force energy.

The thymus gland consists of two lobes and is most prominent during childhood, gradually diminishing in size as we age. It comprises various types of cells, including stem cells, epithelial cells, and T lymphocytes (T cells), which are crucial for immune function.

One of the primary functions of the thymus gland is the maturation and differentiation of T cells. These cells play a vital role in our immune responses, identifying and eliminating foreign pathogens or abnormal cells within the body. The thymus provides an environment for T cells to develop and acquire specific immune functions, contributing to our overall immune system's effectiveness.

Additionally, the thymus gland serves as a regulator of the immune system's activity. It helps distinguish between self and non-self, preventing the immune system from attacking healthy cells and tissues. This regulatory function ensures a balanced immune response, promoting overall health and well-being.

Moreover, the thymus gland is intimately connected to our life force or vital energy. It acts as a reservoir for the life force that flows through the thymus and radiates throughout the body, supporting vitality and optimal functioning. By activating and harnessing this life force within the thymus, profound healing effects can be experienced.

While the thymus gland naturally shrinks as we age, potentially losing some remarkable healing properties, combining specific breathing techniques and activating the Life Force Body can amplify its potential. One such technique is the "Thymus Breath."

To practice Thymus Breathing, find a comfortable sitting position with a straight back. Inhale gently through your nose, simulating a yawn while keeping your mouth closed and your tongue against your palate. Slowly exhale through your nose, again mimicking a yawn. While performing this technique, focus on activating your Life Force Body, as explained in previous chapters, directing your attention towards the thymus gland.

Incorporate a gentle yawn-like effect with each inhalation and exhalation. This yawn-like action helps open and activate the thymus gland. As you engage in this practice, feel the life force flowing from the thymus throughout your body, particularly in the chest area. Repeat this process to establish a strong connection throughout your body. Take as much time as needed and practice this technique frequently.

Approach this practice with objectivity and curiosity, experimenting with it to gauge its effects on your body and experience. It can generate a tangible sensation of life-force energy flowing through the body when performed correctly. The outcomes may vary depending on individual thymus size and response. However, with regular practice, this method can stimulate stem cell production and restore the thymus gland to its optimal size, akin to inflating a balloon.

In conclusion, the heart, the sacred heart symbol, and the thymus gland hold immense significance in various cultural, spiritual, and physiological contexts. Exploring their connections to life force energy, spirituality, and healing potential opens new realms of understanding and possibilities for personal growth and well-being. By recognizing the profound relationship between the sacred heart, thymus gland, and the life force, we unlock a gateway to deeper understanding and transformation. Through activating the Life Force Body and the experience of the flowing liquid metal sensation, we tap into the amplifying power of the sacred heart and the regenerative potential of the thymus gland.

Chapter 9: Stem Cell Production, Genetic Blueprint, Genetics, and Life Force Interplay

In recent years, stem cells' regenerative and healing capabilities have captured significant attention. Stem cells, undifferentiated cells with the unique ability to transform into specialized cell types, play a crucial role in tissue repair, growth, and overall health care.

The production of stem cells within the human body is an intriguing process deeply connected to the concept of the life force. Stem cells can be generated in various tissues and organs throughout the body, contributing to their regenerative capacity. While bone marrow and embryonic tissues have long been recognized as sources of stem cells, we now understand that numerous organs, including the thymus gland, also contain these remarkable cells. The link between stem cell production and the life force lies in the energetic environment of the body. When the life force is abundant and flows harmoniously, it supports optimal cellular function and the production of healthy stem cells. Conversely, imbalances or blockages in the life force can hinder the body's ability to produce and utilize stem cells effectively.

The field of stem cell technology has already demonstrated significant benefits and is now at the forefront of medical research and therapeutic interventions. Stem cell therapies hold immense promise across various medical disciplines due to their unique characteristics and regenerative potential. Like cultivating the life force, these treatments can be used for tissue repair and regeneration. Stem cells can differentiate into diverse cell types within the body, enabling them to regenerate and repair damaged or diseased tissues and organs.

Stem cell therapies have shown potential in treating a wide range of conditions. For instance, they hold promise in addressing spinal cord injuries, heart disease, liver disease, and degenerative joint disorders like osteoarthritis. Stem cell transplants, also known as bone marrow transplants, have been widely employed in treating blood disorders, including leukemia, lymphoma, and certain genetic diseases affecting the blood cells. By transplanting stem cells derived from bone marrow or umbilical cord blood, healthy blood cells can be replenished, and proper immune system functioning can be restored.

In autoimmune diseases, stem cell therapies offer hope by modulating the immune response. These therapies regulate the immune system and reduce inflammation, potentially alleviating conditions such as multiple sclerosis, rheumatoid arthritis, and lupus. Stem cells can also differentiate into neurons and support cells within the central nervous system, opening avenues for treating neurological disorders like Parkinson's disease, Alzheimer's disease, stroke, and spinal cord injuries. By replacing damaged neurons, stimulating tissue repair, and enhancing functional recovery, stem cell therapies aim to improve the lives of individuals affected by these conditions.

Furthermore, stem cells are being explored in cosmetic and reconstructive surgery. They can be utilized in facial rejuvenation, scar revision, wound healing, and tissue grafting, enhancing the natural healing processes and improving outcomes. Both the concept of the life force and stem cell treatments contribute to these remarkable benefits. Although life force and stem cell therapies are distinct concepts, they converge in their focus on harnessing the body's inherent healing capacities.

While exploring these subjects, I came across Tony Robbins's book, LIFE FORCE: How New Breakthroughs in Precision Medicine Can Transform the Quality of Your Life & Those You Love. While I initially anticipated conversations on universal life force energy, the book primarily focuses on the intriguing realm of stem cell technology. Nonetheless, I was amazed by the similarities between stem cell technology and cultivating life force energy.

In the previous chapter, we discovered that T-cells and stem cells can be released by directing our attention and life force energy to the point of, for example, the sacred heart and the thymus gland. Many stem cells can be released within our bodies by inducing a yawning-like breath while activating the Life Force Body. This release is felt from the central point at the sternum, manifesting as a metallic sensation accompanied by a metallic taste. However, it is essential to note that tension around the heart can make this process more challenging, even nearly impossible. We have learned that the thymus gland tends to shrink and become less efficient with age, but it can be revived, much like inflating a balloon. Older individuals with heart problems or who struggle to access their emotions may find this exercise more challenging. Nevertheless, I encourage perseverance and patience. By incorporating practices such as Bhakti Yoga into our lives, we can learn to open our hearts, making the activation of life force energy in and around the heart more accessible.

Reflecting on my personal journey, I grew up in the 1980s when macho behavior was heavily encouraged, and the alpha male archetype was idolized. Films and series like Commando, Predator, He-Man, G.I. Joe, and Conan the Barbarian promoted the idea that expressing emotions was abnormal and weak. The norm was to engage in fights and avoid emotional interactions, especially between boys and girls. These experiences led to a closed heart, rendering it difficult to truly feel. While this mentality proved practical in a reality where fear was a weakness, it presented challenges as I grew older. Acting solely based on reason, without interference from the heart, could make one appear cold, particularly in relationships. Restoring the robust functioning of the thymus gland and the sacred heart can address this limitation. Dedication and perseverance are key elements in this endeavor.

In conclusion, stem cell production within the human body is an intriguing process closely intertwined with the concept of the life force. Stem cell therapies have immense potential in various medical fields owing to their unique regenerative capabilities. As we explore these frontiers, it becomes evident that the life force and stem cell treatments aim to tap into the body's inherent healing capacities. By understanding and nurturing the life force and embracing the remarkable possibilities offered by stem cell technology, we can unlock new dimensions of health, well-being, and transformative medical interventions. Although stem cell technology can significantly contribute to well-being, this book focuses more on repairing the body through cultivating the life force.

9.1 Genetic Blueprint and Its Connection to Vital Force

Observing how our blueprint's information is stored within our DNA is intriguing. The intricate web of life is woven with the threads of genetics, the blueprint that defines the essence of an organism. The genetic code is essential to their existence, from the tiniest microbe to the most intricate multicellular beings. Beyond mere instructions for physical attributes and biological functions lies a more profound connection: the interplay between the genetic blueprint and the enigmatic life force that animates all living things.

Within each cell of every living organism, nestled in the double helix structure of DNA, lies the encoded information that determines form and function. Genes, the segments of DNA, carry the instructions for protein synthesis, the building blocks of life. These proteins coordinate the diverse processes that sustain life, from cellular metabolism to the intricate dance of organ systems.

While DNA is fascinating, especially since much remains an excellent mystery for now, there's the uncoded information and the inactive DNA, also known as JUNK-DNA. What is it, and what can we do with it? I will delve into this topic further in another book titled: "Shapeshifters: A Journey into Multidimensional Consciousness." Regardless, the genetic blueprint serves as a foundation, a canvas upon which the life force paints its masterpiece. It provides the raw materials and the structural framework, while the life force infuses it with vitality and purpose. This relationship is not one of causality but of symbiosis—a dance between the tangible and the intangible, the material and the ethereal.

No matter how deteriorated the body may be, we can breathe life back into its original framework using the energy of the life force. The life force influences gene expression and shapes the development and evolution of an organism. This invisible hand guides the unfolding of genetic potential, steering the course of growth and adaptation. The mysterious power enables regeneration, healing, and the resilience of life in the face of adversity.

In ancient traditions such as Ayurveda, Traditional Chinese Medicine, and various indigenous belief systems, understanding this interplay between the genetic blueprint and the life force forms the basis of holistic healing and well-being. These systems recognize that health is not merely the absence of disease but a state of balance and harmony among an individual's physical, mental, emotional, and spiritual aspects, with the life force as the vital link connecting them all.

While modern science has made remarkable progress in deciphering the genetic code and unraveling the mysteries of life, it is still in the early stages of comprehending the profound relationship between the genetic blueprint and the life force. Research into epigenetics, the study of heritable changes in gene expression that do not involve changes in the underlying DNA sequence, offers glimpses into the intricate interplay between genetics and the environment.

As our understanding deepens, it becomes increasingly clear that the genetic blueprint alone cannot explain life's full complexity and diversity. The life force, that intangible essence weaving the tapestry of existence, remains an alluring enigma that requires further exploration and understanding.

9.2 Unraveling the Interplay between Genetics and Vitality

The human body is a magnificent tapestry of life, inherently woven with the threads of genetics and the ethereal essence of vitality. It is fascinating how these two elements interact with each other, shaping our very existence. From the influence of thoughts and emotions on gene expression to the profound impact of dietary and lifestyle choices, we unveil the hidden secrets of our genetic blueprint and its dynamic relationship with vitality.

At the core of every cell lies the blueprint of life—our DNA—with instructions for development and functioning in every aspect of our being. Traditionally, it was believed that our genetic composition determined our fate and that we were mere pawns in genetics. However, recent breakthroughs in epigenetics have revealed a different truth—the expression of our genes is influenced not only by their inherent code but also by other factors, including our thoughts, emotions, and experiences.

Thoughts and emotions are fleeting phenomena and powerful forces that shape our physiological and psychological well-being. Studies have shown positive emotions, and a healthy mindset can profoundly influence gene expression. I recently read an interesting book, "The Wisdom of Your Cells" by Bruce H. Lipton, which delves further into this topic. I highly recommend it if you're interested in this topic.

A few years ago, a friend and I had our blood checked by an orthomolecular physician. This was through an EMB Blood Test, which stands for "Energetic Morphological Blood Test." This test is offered by some orthomolecular doctors and alternative medical practitioners.

The EMB Blood Test aims to provide information about a person's health by analyzing a drop of dried blood under a microscope. Supporters of the test claim that the blood sample can reveal information about nutrient depletion, digestive issues, toxin burden, and other health problems. Shapes, colors, and patterns of blood cells and other elements in the blood sample can provide clues about the health of various organs and systems in the body that go beyond a regular blood test.

What was intriguing was that the doctor who analyzed my blood also turned out to be highly sensitive, capable of perceiving subtle particles or energies. She predicted that my blood cells could survive for a long time based on my energy field or life force, which was accurate. After witnessing my friend undergo an extensive blood analysis, my blood was taken through a finger prick and examined under a microscope. Her prediction was confirmed again—my blood cells remained vibrant long after the blood draw. Interestingly, my blood differed from my friend's. Notably, there was an abundant amount of oxygen in my blood. Oxygen in the blood is generally beneficial and essential for healthy functioning. Oxygen is necessary for most cells and tissues in the body to function well and produce energy.

Some reasons why sufficient oxygen in the blood is essential include:

- Energy production: Cells in the body require oxygen to produce the energy needed for various biological processes. This energy production occurs in the cell's mitochondria through aerobic respiration.
- Organs and tissues: Organs like the brain, heart, and muscles require a continuous supply of oxygen to function correctly. Oxygen deficiency can lead to reduced performance and, in some cases, tissue damage.
- Circulation: Oxygen is transported to different body parts through red blood cells in the bloodstream. It's essential for delivering oxygen to all cells and removing carbon dioxide, a byproduct of metabolism.

Low oxygen levels in the blood, known as hypoxia, can result in fatigue, dizziness, shortness of breath, and other symptoms. Severe hypoxia can be harmful to vital organs and tissues. Conversely, excessive oxygen levels, as seen in certain medical situations, can also have adverse effects.

Maintaining a healthy balance is crucial, and seeking medical advice is necessary if you suspect any issues with your blood oxygen levels. The elevated oxygen levels in my blood are due to the life force energy. I deliberately experimented with my life force energy to see if it would be observable in my blood, and the answer is yes.

Lipton explains in his book that cells are essentially individuals within a society, each with various tasks, much like our human society. A cell, in itself, is like a mini version of ourselves. In fact, we can extract all the information about who we are from one single cell. It was interesting to observe that my blood cells were incredibly healthy, even though I had previously experienced heart problems due to a blocked artery. This was also detectable in my blood, though I hadn't mentioned it to the orthomolecular physician. This observation was clearly visible on her monitor. Over time, I have addressed this issue by relaxing my heart and allowing life's energy to flow freely. While I used to experience severe heart issues, akin to a series of heart attacks where I sometimes felt disconnected from my body, I am fortunate to no longer experience such problems.

Continuing this journey of exploration, the interconnectedness of our genetic makeup and vitality becomes even more profound. Our bodies are not just passive recipients of gene information but dynamic entities that respond to our thoughts, emotions, and intentions. This intricate dance between our inner world and physical form shapes our health and well-being in ways extending beyond conventional understanding.

As I delved deeper into understanding the interplay between genetics and vitality, I realized the importance of holistic approaches to healthcare. The conventional perspective that genetics solely determine our fate has evolved into a more nuanced understanding that acknowledges the role of epigenetics, environmental factors, and the power of consciousness in shaping our genetic expression.

The EMB Blood Test, guided by the perceptive abilities of the orthomolecular physician, demonstrates the fusion of science and intuition. Witnessing firsthand how the patterns and characteristics of blood cells can provide insights into our health reveals a new dimension of healthcare—one that considers both the physical and energetic aspects of our being.

Incorporating practices that enhance vitality, such as mindfulness, meditation, and life force breathing, takes on a new significance in light of this interconnected perspective. By positively influencing our thoughts and emotions, we can control the expression of our genes, contributing to our overall health and resilience.

My journey of aligning with life force energy and witnessing its impact on my blood vitality has strengthened my belief in the intricate relationship between our inner and outer worlds. The transformation from experiencing heart issues to finding balance and well-being has underscored the potential for healing within us. It's a testament to the power of conscious intention and the body's capacity to respond to positive shifts in energy and mindset.

In essence, unraveling the interplay between genetics and vitality invites us to explore the depths of our existence. It encourages us to step beyond the boundaries of traditional medicine and embrace a more holistic approach—one that considers the unity of mind, body, and the life force. As we continue to unveil the mysteries of our genetic blueprint and its dance with vitality, we embark on a journey of self-discovery and empowerment, harnessing the immense potential within us to shape our health and well-being in profound ways.

Chapter 10: Focused Awareness, Enhancing Memory, and Observed Reality

Maintaining focus is more crucial than ever in today's fast-paced, distraction-filled society. The demands for our attention are constant, and it is easy to get pulled in countless directions, hindering our ability to achieve our desires and turn them into successes. Whether striving to work on ourselves through introspection or building a striving future, a strong sense of focus is essential. Through this focused awareness, the life force energy within us begins to circulate, propelling us forward and enhancing our ability to concentrate.

Life is a complex tapestry of roles and responsibilities, each requiring our attention and energy. Therefore, finding balance and harmony is crucial, whether the relationships we build, the work we engage in, or our pursuit of personal goals. In this journey, the power of the dynamic life force intertwines with our focused awareness, guiding us toward transformation and success.

Cultivating the life force within us enables us to be more present and engaged in every aspect of our lives. It means fully immersed in the present moment, free from distractions and external influences that might pull us away. By embracing the life force, we unlock the potential to create harmony externally and within ourselves as we tap into our profound energy.

One area where focused awareness can profoundly enhance our lives is our relationships. In today's fast-paced world, it is easy to be physically present but mentally absent when interacting with others. However, when we cultivate focused awareness and harness the life force in our connections, we bring depth and meaning to each interaction. Genuine listening, empathetic understanding, and authentic presence build stronger bonds and foster open communication. By integrating the life force into our relationships, we become more patient, focused, and capable of enriching our connections on a deeper level.

The influence of focused awareness extends beyond our personal lives and professional endeavors. Recognizing the power of concentrated attention is crucial in a society that values multitasking and constant busyness. The life force becomes the fuel that energizes our efforts, providing vitality and inspiration as we navigate our path with clarity and purpose. We unlock heightened efficiency, creativity, and problem-solving abilities by channeling the life force into our work. Fully immersed in the present moment, we transcend time constraints and external pressures, unleashing our full potential for personal and professional growth. This cultivation of the life force illuminates our journey toward our goals and aspirations, propelling us forward with unwavering determination.

In the vastness of our dreams, it is easy to become overwhelmed or distracted by external influences. However, we can make significant progress by anchoring ourselves to the life force. Aligning our focused awareness with the power of the life force allows us to break down our goals into manageable tasks, cultivate resilience in the face of obstacles, and celebrate each small victory. The life force becomes the guiding light that propels us forward, infusing our actions with intention and purpose.

10.1 Enhancing Memory through Vital Life Energy

The vital energy is a captivating phenomenon that holds the potential to significantly enrich our lives, depending on how we channel this energy to impact both body and mind. When vitality energy is concentrated within the mind, it inevitably influences our brain's capacity, including its impact on memory. Some studies have measured the brain's ability based on the energy it receives. In other words, the more life force energy, the more effectively the brain functions.

Neuroscientific studies have also begun to scratch the surface of how vital energy interacts with the human brain. Advanced imaging techniques have revealed that those with a more balanced energy flow have increased activity in the prefrontal cortex, an area of the brain associated with planning, decision-making, and emotional regulation.

Moreover, specific research indicates that individuals regularly engage in energy-balancing practices have enhanced neural plasticity, facilitating better learning and adaptability.

Furthermore, this life force energy doesn't only influence cognitive functions. It plays a pivotal role in our overall well-being. When the energy flows freely, there's a reduction in physical ailments and emotional disturbances. On the contrary, blockages or imbalances in this energy often manifest as illnesses, fatigue, or even psychological disorders.

I once read somewhere that when we lose something, like a set of keys, it's better to focus on where they might be for a short time. Instead, we should focus on other activities, allowing the subconscious to search for the keys while we engage in different tasks. The subconscious mind utilizes a significantly more considerable

brain capacity than our conscious mind.
This approach can lead to sudden insights
into where we lost items. I've tested this
method numerous times, and it holds some
truth. However, there are also other
techniques to tap into our memory easily.

Once we become acquainted with the vital
force, we must channel it within our minds
while visually exploring our memory.
Everything becomes considerably clearer,
making tasks like locating our keys, for
example, much more straightforward. It's
also intriguing to revisit specific moments
from the past using the power of life force.
I've often wondered about individuals with
a photographic memory – why can they
remember everything in such intricate detail
while others struggle with this ability? Isn't
something like this accessible to everyone?
After all, we are all human beings capable of
such extraordinary feats. I'm convinced that
this vitality energy is critical in memory and
cognitive capacities, serving as the key to

numerous aspects. Ultimately, it's about nurturing the life force.

I challenge you to engage in a fun exercise. Close your eyes and recall a random event while channeling energy into your mind. Feel how this experience resonates with you. You might sense this energy in a specific brain area where memories are stored. This sensation can be interpreted in various ways, including resistance or mild discomfort. However, this is a positive sign, as it expands our mental horizons. Keep your eyes closed as you feel the vital life energy multiplying within your mind. While still keeping your eyes shut, contemplate this event. Do you notice new details or things you initially forgot? Can you perceive the difference between when energy is channeled and when it's not? The more we engage in this practice, the more refined it becomes. It's a form of brain training utilizing the power of vitality energy.

As we delve deeper into the realm of memory enhancement through the utilization of vital life energy, we unlock a doorway to a more profound connection with our past experiences. This practice not only aids in retrieving forgotten details but also fosters a heightened awareness and understanding of the events that have shaped us.

Imagine the potential applications of this technique – not just for locating lost objects or recalling past events but also for boosting creativity and problem-solving skills. By channeling the vital energy and directing it towards specific memories or challenges, we could tap into the vast knowledge and insights in our minds.

Furthermore, cultivating this energy for memory enhancement opens the door to a holistic approach to mental well-being. Just as we exercise our bodies to keep them healthy, we can exercise our minds by focusing or channeling this vital life energy. "Where the intention goes, the energy flows."

The optimal approach is to thoroughly circulate the vital energy throughout the body. As we see with the Life Force Body. This practice aligns with ancient traditions that have long recognized mind, body, and spirit interconnectedness.

Consider the implications for individuals who have struggled with memory-related issues, such as cognitive decline or learning difficulties. While this approach isn't a cure-all per se, it offers a potential path for improvement that completes existing methods and therapies.

As with any other practice, consistency is critical. The more we channel vital energy, the more attuned we become to its effects. Over time, we may notice an overall improvement in cognitive functions beyond memory alone. It's as if we are unlocking hidden potential within ourselves, unveiling a reservoir of mental abilities that were always present but not fully tapped into.

In conclusion, exploring memory enhancement through the utilization of vital life energy is an exciting journey into the capabilities of our own minds. Integrating this practice into our lives enhances our memory and deepens our connection with ourselves and the world around us. It's a reminder that the human mind remains a frontier filled with untapped potential, waiting to be discovered and harnessed for our own benefit.

10.2 Observed Reality

Quantum physicists have discovered that quantum particles react differently when observed, a phenomenon that has puzzled the scientific community. This experiment is one of the most well-known and fundamental experiments in quantum mechanics, with significant implications for our understanding of the nature of reality, also known as the double-slit experiment.

In the double-slit experiment, a source of particles, such as electrons or photons, is directed towards a screen with two narrow slits. Behind the screen, a detection screen is placed to observe the arrival of the particles. When the particles are fired without observation, they are expected to exhibit an interference pattern on the detection screen, similar to the interference of waves. This suggests that the particles behave like waves and pass through both slits simultaneously.

However, when an observation is made to determine which slit a particle passes through, such as by placing measuring devices at the slits, the behavior of the particles changes. Instead of displaying an interference pattern, they behave as particles and show a way as if they passed through only one of the slits. The act of observation seems to "collapse" the particle's wave-like behavior and forces it to behave as a particle with a specific location.

This phenomenon, known as the "observer effect" in quantum mechanics, has intrigued scientists for years and has led to various interpretations and discussions about the nature of reality and the role of the observer in the quantum mechanical system. The experiment highlights the non-intuitive nature of quantum mechanics and the challenges in understanding the fundamental nature of matter and energy at the subatomic level.

Several interpretations and explanations have been proposed to understand the observer effect, such as the Copenhagen interpretation, the many-worlds interpretation, and the pilot-wave theory.

Each of these interpretations has its own approach and implications for our understanding of quantum mechanics and the nature of reality. However, scientists still need to agree on which performance provides the most accurate description of the phenomenon. It remains an active area of research in which scientists strive for a deeper understanding of quantum mechanics and its implications for our perception of the world around us.

One thing is clear, though, that consciousness does impact physical matter. This reminds me of a Zen quote or koan that explores the nature of perception and reality. It is the question: "If a tree falls in the forest and no one is around to hear it, does it make a sound?"

This question is intended to challenge assumptions and concepts about perception and reality. It calls for self-inquiry and invites us to question our assumptions about the world. It invites us to contemplate the nature of sound, perception, and the role of the observer in creating our experiences.

This Zen koan is not meant to find a specific answer but to open our minds to the mysterious nature of reality. It emphasizes the importance of direct experience and letting go of concepts and judgments to see the truth as it is without interfering with our thinking.

Meditating on this koan frees the mind from dualistic concepts and allows us to experience what is without the filter of our ego or intellect. It invites us to expand our consciousness and discover that the boundary between the observing subject and the observed object is ultimately one and the same or illusory. This reminds me of the term "rendering" in the context of the simulation hypothesis.

The simulation hypothesis is that our reality, including the entire universe and everything within it, could be an artificial simulation created by an advanced civilization or a higher entity. The idea suggests that the physical world around us is a complex computer-generated simulation, similar to a video game or virtual reality. We don't live in a virtual world, but the nature of reality is more holographic than solid.

Rendering, in this context, is similar to the rendering process in computer graphics, where a virtual scene is converted into a visual representation that can be perceived by an observer. In a simulated reality, the rendering process would involve generating sensory input, such as visual, auditory, tactile, and other sensations that individuals within the simulation experience.

According to the simulation hypothesis, the simulated reality would only need to be rendered when necessary for an observer or conscious being within the simulation to perceive or interact with a specific aspect of the simulated world. This concept is often associated with "rendering on demand," where computational power is given to render particular parts of the simulated environment when they come into focus or become relevant to the experiences of conscious beings or observed reality.

I have conducted extensive research on parallel worlds theoretically and through direct experience, also known as quantum jumping. Quantum jumping refers to the idea that individuals can consciously "jump" between different parallel worlds or realities to experience life changes.

According to these ideas, quantum jumping involves using consciousness, intention, or visualization to shift to an alternative reality where desired changes or circumstances occur. It is often seen as a way to become a better version of oneself, choose a different career path, improve health, or achieve other desired goals. I have experienced many bizarre and extraordinary things, especially when I make a dimension shift within myself. I have seen the world around me change immediately after drastic changes within myself. For example, the sun suddenly starts shining from stormy weather outside, various opportunities arise, or synchronicities occur. I have even seen things of unexplained origin or parallel realities.

What does this have to do with the life force? Well, the life force is a tool we can use to shape life and ourselves. When activating the Life Force Body energy, we can multiply the quality of life by letting it flow within us.

In a previous chapter, we discussed pain and the life force, wherein we embrace pain and all discomfort within ourselves. This is crucial and often overlooked. We tend to hold onto specific structures or patterns, creating tension. Life force energy gives us the courage to observe and transcend these patterns within ourselves, resulting in a healthier, better appearance and a prosperous life.

When we can consciously expand the life force energy far beyond the body, we can transcend the discomfort outside ourselves and influence the world around us. Just as in the double-slit experiment, particles react differently when observed. The world responds differently when our life force and attention remain strong enough.

Lastly, the world is different from what people generally think it is. Reality is, in fact, inherently illusory, also known as Maya. The concept of Maya originally comes from ancient Hinduism, one of the oldest religions in the world. The idea of Maya is discussed and refined in these scriptures. One of the key texts that address the concept of Maya is the "Vedanta" or "Upanishads." These texts form the philosophical foundation of Hinduism and contain discussions on the nature of reality, the self, and the illusory nature of the world. This also reminds me of the Hermetic principles.

The Hermetic principles are philosophical concepts that originated in Hermetism, an ancient spiritual tradition attributed to Hermes Trismegistus, a mythical figure who's a great teacher and sage. These principles provide insights and guidelines for understanding the workings of the universe and the relationship between humans and the cosmos. Let's compare these principles to the observed reality:

1. The Principle of Mentalism states that the universe has a mental nature and that everything is essentially thoughts or consciousness. In observed reality,

we can see that our thoughts and consciousness significantly influence our experiences and perceptions. Our thoughts and beliefs affect how we perceive the world around us and how we interact with it.

2. The Principle of Correspondence: This principle states that there are similarities and analogies between different levels of reality. What happens at the microscopic level may be similar to what happens at the macroscopic level. In observed reality, we see this principle in action in disciplines such as quantum mechanics, where the properties of particles at the microscopic level can be similar to those of objects at the macroscopic level.

3. The Principle of Vibration: This principle states that everything in the universe vibrates and is in motion. At the subatomic level, matter and

energy consist of vibrating particles. We can perceive these vibrations in observed reality, such as sound, light, and electromagnetic waves.

4. The Principle of Polarity: This principle states that everything in the universe has polarities, opposite poles that complement and need each other for their existence. In observed reality, we see polarity in concepts such as heat and cold, inside and outside, light and dark, and positive and negative. These opposite poles create balance and harmony in the world around us.

5. The Principle of Rhythm states that everything in the universe moves cyclically and in rhythm. Observed reality demonstrates this principle in seasons, day and night, and ebb and flow. Everything has its own rhythm and movement.

6. The Principle of Cause and Effect: This
   principle states that every cause has
   an effect, and every effect has a cause.
   In observed reality, we can see this
   principle in the laws of physics, where
   action and reaction follow each other.
   Every action has consequences, and
   every event has a cause.
7. The Principle of Gender: This
   principle states that everything in the
   universe has masculine and feminine
   elements, which complement and
   need each other for creation and
   reproduction. In observed reality, we
   see this principle in action in
   biological reproduction and the
   creation of new life forms.

Although the Hermetic principles form a
profound and extensive philosophy, we can
perceive and recognize elements of these
principles in the reality around us. They
provide a framework for expanding our
perception of the world and understanding

the underlying patterns and processes that influence reality.

We see a recurring theme in which consciousness influences physical reality. Combining these principles with the life force can drastically affect our strength and vitality and shape our world. The life force enables us to create the life that suits us. This requires awareness of internal processes and blockages to transcend them if necessary.

During a car ride to Antwerp, I received a spontaneous telepathic message from my extraterrestrial guides. It happens sometimes. This time, they told me there is no such thing as a time buffer for manifesting. We experience a time buffer because we cling to familiar patterns. When our reality drastically distorts, fear of the unknown arises, and we fall back into old habits or patterns. They explained that we must embrace everything within ourselves, regardless of the external world, even if it seems like the end of the world.

Later, when I was in Egypt, somewhere in a typical authentic alley where a lot was happening, I decided to examine this further. At first, everything was chaotic, as it can be in Egypt. People were begging, merchants, people with leprosy, stray dogs, disabled individuals, waitresses, dancers, people arguing, shopkeepers, tourists passing by - all sorts of things. I sat on a terrace, enjoying an Egyptian cup of tea while observing the surroundings. It was chaotic - a perfect moment to put the insights from my extraterrestrial friends into practice by embracing everything within myself. I literally saw the world around me change immediately. People arguing started to laugh, and the environment transformed into a festive atmosphere. So much happened in just 5 minutes, and my senses were pleasantly stimulated. I had never experienced anything like this before. Even

the Egyptians I was with, who had grown
up and lived in that environment, were
amazed. Despite being familiar with the
surroundings, this was their first time
witnessing something like this. Indeed,
consciousness has an impact on the
environment. This was just one of the
countless times I've seen my surroundings
dramatically change instantaneously,
usually when I undergo a shift in
consciousness within myself.

Another moment, while wandering through
the Dutch meadows in the evening, I
pondered what it would be like if there
were a star gate where you could pass
through and end up somewhere else, much
like in the movie "Stargate." To my great
surprise, not even a minute later, I saw a
gigantic star gate in the distance, just like
the one from the movie "Stargate," parked
next to the highway. It was at least 10 meters
tall! I couldn't believe my eyes; I had never
seen anything like it. It would take at least

half an hour to walk it through the
meadows, and I planned to check it out the
next day. However, I regretted it afterward
because it was gone the next day. I could
write an entire book about such experiences.
The point is that the world is not what we
think it is, and consciousness can influence
the reality around us. However, life force
energy can play an essential role and a
missing link in shaping our reality.

Chapter 11: Concentrated Life Force in Food, Medical and Psychedelic Mushrooms

We can modify our diets to tap into a more profound life force. While the life force from nutrition isn't critical, it is still essential. Techniques like pranayama are prioritized because they target the primary source of life force. Nonetheless, food is necessary as it gives our bodies the energy to operate.

Consider the analogy of blueberries and french fries. Blueberries are rich in vital energy or life force, while french fries lack this essential essence. We consume the life force inherent in food through our meals and drinks. We also breathe in this vital energy in varying quantities.

However, food holds a more profound significance beyond mere nourishment. It is a conduit for life force energy, influencing our physical, mental, and spiritual well-being. Throughout history, cultures have recognized the connection between the life force within food and its potential to nourish and heal our bodies. Specific foods can enhance vitality, promote balance, and elevate consciousness. Certain foods are to possess higher life force energy or vibrations. These foods are typically fresh, organic, and minimally processed, preserving natural energy. Fruits, vegetables, whole grains, nuts, seeds, and plant-based foods are generally known for their high vibrational properties.

Conversely, heavily processed, chemically filled, and artificial foods have a lower life force, providing little nourishment beyond primary care. In many ancient cultures, food preparation was considered a sacred ritual that infused the meal with positive intentions and prayers. When prepared with love, gratitude, and mindfulness, the cook imbues the food with positive energy, elevating its life force and enhancing nutrient absorption for those who consume it.

Traditional Practices and Their Wisdom: Throughout history, cultures worldwide have developed practices and dietary guidelines that align with the concept of concentrated life force in food. For example, Ayurveda, an ancient Indian system of medicine, emphasizes eating according to one's dosha (body type) to maintain balance and harmony. Similarly, Traditional Chinese Medicine (TCM) focuses on the energetic properties of food and how it affects the body's organs and meridians. Certain foods possess specific life-enhancing properties. Superfoods like spirulina, chlorella, and wheatgrass are rich in chlorophyll and antioxidants, thought to cleanse and energize the body. Moreover, herbs and spices like turmeric, ginger, and garlic are valued for their healing and immunity-boosting properties.

Raw and living foods like sprouts, fruits, and vegetables are potent carriers of life force energy. The life force is more vibrant and active in these uncooked and unprocessed foods, providing the body with easily assimilated nutrients and enzymes.

Conscious eating involves being fully present and aware of our food. By cultivating mindful eating practices, we can better connect with the life force within our food and honor the sustenance it provides. Slowing down, savoring each bite, and expressing gratitude can amplify the energetic benefits of the meal.

A human can easily go weeks without food, only a few days without water, but not a moment without the life force energy.

Healthy eating is therefore secondary, with water or life force cultivation being primary.

For many spiritual traditions, food serves as physical nourishment and a means to elevate consciousness and forge a deeper connection with the divine. Vegetarian and plant-based diets are often encouraged and believed to support a more precise and more refined spiritual awareness.

In conclusion, the concept of concentrated life force in food transcends cultural boundaries, reflecting the profound interplay between what we consume and our well-being. Embracing high-vibration foods, preparing meals with positive intentions, and cultivating mindful eating practices can harness the concentrated life force in food to support our physical health, mental clarity, and spiritual growth. By recognizing the significance of the life force within our nourishment, we align ourselves with the natural rhythms of the universe, embracing the vitality and vibrancy that nourishes our entire being.

11.1 Medical Mushrooms and the Life Force: Unlocking Nature's Healing Power

In the mystical realm of the forest floor, beneath the dappled sunlight and amongst the whispering leaves, a profound secret of healing lies in the intricate world of medical mushrooms. These fascinating fungi, long revered by ancient cultures for their therapeutic properties, hold within them a potent life force that transcends the boundaries of the natural world. As we delve into the enchanting world of medical mushrooms, we unveil the mystique surrounding their life-enhancing essence, igniting the profound connection between these humble organisms and the life force that sustains us all.

For millennia, civilizations across the globe have cherished medicinal mushrooms as sacred gifts from the earth. In the heart of traditional Chinese medicine, revered mushrooms like Reishi, Cordyceps, and Shiitake have been venerated for their ability to restore harmony and balance within the body. Ancient healers and shamans recognized the life force energy that pulsates within these fungi, harnessing their power to treat myriad ailments, nourish vitality, and cultivate spiritual well-being.

Embodying the essence of immortality, Reishi, or the "Mushroom of Immortality," symbolizes profound reverence and healing in Eastern cultures. With its woody texture and bitter taste, Reishi contains a treasure trove of bioactive compounds, including triterpenes, polysaccharides, and antioxidants. These elements synergistically support the immune system, reduce inflammation, and enhance overall vitality.

The life force energy of Reishi permeates the body, nourishing the soul and invoking a sense of grounded tranquility that transcends time.

As if ingrained with the essence of boundless energy, Cordyceps mushrooms sprout forth from the Himalayan foothills, captivating the hearts of ancient Tibetan healers. These unique fungi are renowned for their energy-boosting properties to enhance stamina, endurance, and oxygen utilization. Cordyceps' life force energy flows through the body, revitalizing both mind and muscles and empowering individuals to reach new heights of physical and mental performance.

Amidst the lush woodlands of Japan, the Shiitake mushroom stands as a symbol of vitality and rejuvenation. Rich in immune-enhancing beta-glucans and essential vitamins, Shiitake supports cardiovascular health and boosts the body's defense mechanisms. Its life force energy nurtures the essence of life within, promoting resilience and vitality while embodying the profound interconnectedness between the natural world and human existence.

In the heart of the ancient forests, a mystical and elusive organism thrives, holding within its woody essence the captivating secret of the life force that pulses through the natural world. The Chaga mushroom, often called the "King of Mushrooms," is a majestic guardian of vitality and a potent carrier of life force energy. Revered for centuries by indigenous cultures and traditional healers, the Chaga mushroom's enigmatic properties have earned it a place of honor in natural medicine and holistic healing.

The Lion's Mane mushroom is a unique and striking organism, resembling a cascading waterfall of icicles or a snow-white lion's mane. Unlike traditional mushrooms, it lacks a cap and stems, growing in a cascading, shaggy formation that captivates our imagination. Often found on hardwood trees like beech, oak, and maple, Lion's Mane is a master of adaptation, harmonizing with its surroundings and weaving a symbiotic relationship with the living trees.

The Life Force within the Lion's Mane Mushroom:

Ancient cultures revered the Lion's Mane mushroom as a symbol of vitality and renewal, attributing its unique appearance to the presence of the life force that permeates the natural world. Within its pristine, ivory-white fibers lies a concentrated essence of the life force harnessed from the living trees it calls home. As it draws upon the vital energy of the forest, the Lion's Mane mushroom becomes a vessel of regeneration and healing, embodying the interconnectedness of all living beings.

Modern scientific research continues to unveil the secrets behind the magic of medical mushrooms and their life-enhancing properties. Studies have validated their immune-modulating, anti-inflammatory, and antioxidant effects, solidifying their role as nature's potent healers. As we delve into the molecular intricacies of these fungi, we encounter the essence of life force energy encoded within their cellular structures.

11.2 Psychedelic Mushrooms and the Life Force: Unveiling the Mysteries of Consciousness

I have noticed that psychedelic mushrooms contain an immense life force energy, which can be felt even from a few meters away. This becomes especially evident when you work extensively with life force energy. Although psychedelic mushrooms are often associated with drugs, they possess medicinal properties. Despite controversial opinions, there is a growing interest in the potential medical benefits of psychedelic mushrooms, particularly in treating conditions such as depression, anxiety disorders, and post-traumatic stress disorder (PTSD). Clinical trials and studies have demonstrated promising results of psilocybin, the primary psychoactive compound in magic mushrooms, in treating depression.

Psilocybin has a unique effect on the brain, particularly on the serotonin system. It influences serotonin receptors, a neurotransmitter crucial to mood, emotions, and cognitive functions. Through its interaction with these receptors, psilocybin can induce various effects that impact mental well-being.

In recent years, various hospitals and research institutions worldwide have shown interest in using psychedelic mushrooms, especially psilocybin, as a potential treatment for depression and other mental disorders. Researchers have conducted clinical trials to explore the safety and effectiveness of psilocybin in depression treatment, and some hospitals have carried out these studies under controlled conditions.

The use of psychedelic mushrooms in hospitals occurs in a clinical setting where participants are guided by trained professionals. The environment is carefully crafted to promote a positive and supportive experience. This often involves creating a comfortable, tranquil space and providing emotional support. Usually, such sessions occur once a month, and patients may no longer need regular medication.

In the chapter on chakras, we discussed the functioning of these energy centers in the body and mind. Chakras play a significant role in bridging the metaphysical and physical worlds. In another chapter, "Observed Reality," we learned that we are intricately connected to the world and that the body is part of a larger whole. From a holistic perspective, when we take psychedelic mushrooms (in a proper setting), our minds expand because the life force is so intense that all our chakras open up, granting us access to the bigger picture. This is why it is called a mind-expanding substance. A "bad trip" essentially arises from wanting to control the experience because when our perception begins to change, it can be frightening, primarily due to fear of the unknown. This need for control causes us to cling to old habits and patterns within ourselves, which narrows the life force due to the tension within us, resulting in what they call a "bad trip." The only control we can genuinely exercise during such a trip is to let go of control, which is what it's all about. It's like the analogy of a floating cork going with the river's flow.

Dating back to the dawn of civilization, psychedelic mushrooms have been revered as sacred gifts from the earth, portals to the realm of the divine, and conduits to the life force that flows through all living beings. Ancient cultures, such as the Aztecs, Mayans, and indigenous tribes, incorporated these transformative fungi into their spiritual practices, using them as tools for communion with the gods, healers, and spiritual guides. The wisdom of the ancients recognized that psychedelic mushrooms contained a mystical life force energy capable of unlocking hidden dimensions of consciousness.

The psychedelic experience often leads to a profound sense of expanded consciousness, dissolving the illusory boundaries that separate the self from others and fostering a deep recognition of the interconnectedness of all life. In this state of heightened awareness, individuals may experience a profound communion with nature, the cosmos, and the essence of the life force that pulsates through every atom of existence. Psychedelic mushrooms can remind us that we are all integral parts of the universal dance, interconnected threads woven into the cosmic fabric of creation.

Beyond the veil of perception lies the potential for profound healing and transformation. Many individuals report therapeutic and healing effects from their psychedelic experiences, claiming relief from anxiety, depression, and emotional traumas. The profound introspection and the dissolution of ego barriers during these experiences can catalyze profound shifts in consciousness, paving the way for self-acceptance, personal growth, and a deeper connection to the life force energy that flows through the core of our being.

Psychedelic mushrooms hold great power and must be approached with respect and intention. Responsible use in safe and supportive settings is essential to harnessing the full potential of the psychedelic experience.

Although psychedelics can act as mind openers or teachers, as they always provide us what we need at the right moment, the key lies in integrating these teachings into everyday life. The integration offers the opportunity to nurture a deeper connection with the life force energy and to apply the wisdom gained from the mystical realm to the challenges and joys of human existence.

Chapter 12: The Positive Effects of Fasting, Detox and Life Force

Fasting, an age-old practice observed by diverse cultures and religions, involves voluntarily abstaining from food or drink for a specific period. Beyond its traditional spiritual significance, fasting has gained profound recognition in modern times for its potential positive effects on the body and mind. Moreover, supporters of fasting firmly believe in its ability to foster a deeper connection with the life force. In this exploration, we will delve into the undeniable positive effects of fasting and how it can unlock the gateway to the life force and personal transformation. I have practiced fasting throughout my life, which has been a positive experience. One of the primary reasons for fasting is to provide the body with a reset. By giving it time to recover, we allow the body to heal, which is crucial, especially in today's age of overconsumption. We often eat more than our bodies can handle, as consuming multiple meals and snacks throughout the day has become commonplace. Nearly all the food and drinks available for purchase are filled with various additives, known as E-numbers, or genetically modified food, which can harm our health in the long run.

While some E-numbers may not be harmful, certain combinations and quantities can negatively impact the body. This difficulty in recovery increases the likelihood of aging and developing diseases. Therefore, fasting can significantly contribute to a prosperous life.

In addition to providing the body an opportunity to detoxify and rejuvenate, fasting can also help promote mindful eating habits. It allows individuals to become more aware of their dietary choices and their effects on their bodies. By breaking free from the norm of constant eating, we gain a new perspective on our relationship with food and, therefore, develop healthier eating habits.

Moreover, fasting has been shown to have various health benefits, such as improved insulin sensitivity, reduced inflammation, and enhanced brain function. These positive effects can lead to a higher quality of life and a decreased risk of chronic diseases.

Approaching fasting with proper knowledge and guidance is essential, ensuring it is done safely and effectively. Consulting a healthcare professional or a nutritionist can help tailor a fasting plan that best suits individual needs and goals.

In conclusion, incorporating fasting into our lives can offer a much-needed pause for our bodies to heal and reset. In the face of our current culture of overconsumption and processed foods, fasting provides a valuable opportunity to prioritize our health and well-being. By embracing fasting as a part of a holistic lifestyle, we can foster a sense of well-being, reduce the risk of illness, and pave the way for a thriving life.

For centuries, fasting has been an integral part of human history, woven into the fabric of various cultural and religious traditions. While its roots lie in spiritual and religious practices, modern research has revealed numerous benefits fasting grants to our physical and mental well-being. In this chapter, we embark on a journey to uncover the remarkable advantages of fasting, detoxing, life force, and its profound impact on overall health.

Among its most well-known benefits, fasting has shown exceptional effectiveness in helping weight management. By limiting the eating window and reducing calorie intake, fasting induces a calorie deficiency, facilitating weight loss. Additionally, fasting stimulates the production of human growth hormone (HGH), which aids in fat-burning and preserving lean muscle mass.

Another impressive benefit of fasting is its ability to positively impact insulin sensitivity and blood sugar regulation. By granting the pancreas a much-needed break from constant insulin production, fasting improves glucose control and reduces the risk of type 2 diabetes.

Delving into the cellular level, fasting triggers a state of autophagy—a process that entails the removal of damaged cells and recycling their components. This crucial cellular repair mechanism slows aging and lowers the risk of age-related diseases.

Moreover, fasting promotes the production of brain-derived neurotrophic factor (BDNF), a protein that nurtures the growth and maintenance of neurons. Elevated BDNF levels are associated with enhanced brain function, improved cognitive abilities, and a decreased risk of neurodegenerative diseases such as Alzheimer's and Parkinson's.

Beyond its physical benefits, fasting augments the body's metabolic flexibility, enabling it to efficiently switch between burning carbohydrates and fats for energy. This metabolic adaptability contributes to increased energy levels and endurance during physical activities.

Fasting also exhibits a powerful anti-inflammatory effect, reducing markers of inflammation in the body and bolstering the immune system. By mitigating chronic inflammation, fasting diminishes the risk of various inflammatory-related conditions, including cardiovascular disease and arthritis.

Intermittent fasting, in particular, emerges as a potent ally in supporting heart health. By improving blood pressure, cholesterol levels, and other cardiovascular risk factors, fasting significantly reduces the likelihood of heart-related issues.

Mentally, fasting bestows a heightened sense of clarity and focus as the body is unburdened from constant food digestion. Many individuals report experiencing increased alertness and improved concentration during fasting periods.

Moreover, fasting gives the digestive system much-needed rest, shifting energy towards vital processes. This cleansing effect allows the body to detoxify, purging accumulated waste and toxins and leaving individuals feeling rejuvenated and attuned to their bodies.

As individuals embark on fasting journeys, they often become more mindful of their body's sensations and needs. This heightened awareness fosters a deeper connection with one's inner self and leads to improved self-care practices.

In a surprising twist, fasting leads to increased energy levels and an overall sense of vitality. When the body is free from digestion, it can redirect its resources toward cellular repair and regeneration, promoting an overwhelming sense of well-being and stamina.

Beyond the physical and mental realms, fasting acts as an emotional cleanse, allowing suppressed emotions to surface and be released. As individuals delve into the depths of their consciousness, they may experience emotional breakthroughs, leading to a sense of emotional clarity and inner peace.

For those who embrace spiritual beliefs, fasting can be a profound pathway to deepen their connection with the life force. Many view fasting as a means to align themselves with this cosmic energy, fostering a sense of deep interconnectedness.

Embracing fasting requires immense self-discipline and willpower, as individuals must resist the urge to indulge in food. Consequently, fasting instills a profound sense of inner strength and resilience, empowering individuals to overcome challenges in other aspects of life.

As fasting invites individuals to confront their physical and emotional limitations, it simultaneously opens the gateway to self-discovery and transformation. Fasting is not merely an ancient practice but a powerful gateway to unlocking the potential of our bodies, minds, and spirits. Its myriad positive effects on physical health, mental clarity, and emotional well-being make fasting an extraordinary tool for personal growth and a profound connection with the life force that flows through all existence. Embracing fasting as a regular practice can lead us to unleash our inner power and embrace the fullness of life.

12.1 Natural Detoxing

Detoxification, the ancient practice of purging toxins and harmful substances from the body, has deep roots in diverse cultures and traditions. While this ritual was once understood as a crucial element for maintaining optimal health, our modern lifestyle has exposed us to an overwhelming influx of environmental impurities and processed foods, challenging our natural detoxification mechanisms. In exploring detoxing and its profound connection to the life force, we will uncover its transformative power, revitalizing our physical well-being and nurturing our mental and spiritual dimensions.

The present era of industrialization and uncontrolled chemical usage relentlessly subjects our bodies to toxins from multiple sources - the air we breathe, the food we consume, and the products we use. As these harmful substances accumulate over time, our natural detoxification pathways become overburdened, leading to various health problems. The essence of detoxification is to assist the body in ridding itself of these accumulated toxins, thus restoring balance and harmony.

We delved into fasting and its remarkable effects, which include detoxification. However, fasting is just one among many detoxification methods available to us. A common and highly effective approach is dietary Detox, where we adjust our diet to focus on whole, organic foods rich in antioxidants, vitamins, and minerals. Emphasizing fresh fruits, vegetables, and leafy greens can significantly support liver function and aid in the elimination of toxins. On the contrary, minimizing processed foods, sugary beverages, and alcohol can help reduce the burden of toxins on the body.

Hydration is another crucial aspect of detoxification. Staying adequately hydrated enables the body to flush toxins through urine and sweat. Adding a squeeze of lemon to our water can further enhance detoxification, as lemons possess natural cleansing properties.

For those seeking a more intensive approach, juice cleanses offer an opportunity to flood the body with nutrient-rich fruit and vegetable juices. This influx of vitamins and antioxidants can be particularly beneficial for supporting liver function and enhancing the body's detoxification efforts. However, caution must be exercised during juice cleanses, as they may lack essential nutrients and lead to calorie deficiency if not carefully managed.

Furthermore, herbal detox methods offer a natural way to aid the body's cleansing processes. Incorporating herbs like milk thistle, dandelion root, and cilantro into our diet or supplements can provide valuable support in removing heavy metals and enhancing detoxification.

Regular exercise plays a pivotal role in stimulating blood circulation and lymphatic flow, effectively assisting the elimination of toxins through sweat and respiration. Engaging in activities such as yoga, jogging, or strength training can significantly contribute to overall health and facilitate the detoxification process.

Additionally, techniques like dry brushing can be employed to gently stimulate the skin's lymphatic system, promoting the removal of waste and toxins from the body. Colon cleansing methods, such as enemas, colon hydrotherapy, or herbal supplements, help flush out accumulated waste and toxins from the colon, further aiding the detoxification process.

While detoxification is often associated with the physical body, it also encompasses emotional well-being. Mindfulness, meditation, energetic cleansing, and talk therapy are valuable tools for releasing emotional baggage and reducing stress, constituting an emotional detox.

Moreover, a digital detox, involving periodic breaks from digital devices and screens, can alleviate stress, improve sleep quality, and promote mental clarity.

Sauna therapy is another effective method of activating the body's natural detoxification process. Spending time in a sauna induces sweating, expelling heavy metals and other toxins through the skin.

While sauna therapy activates the natural detoxification process, I want to emphasize that we can achieve the same effects through a specific meditation technique. This reminds me of tummo, also known as inner fire meditation or psychic heat meditation, a unique and advanced practice originating from the Tibetan Buddhist tradition. It is a form of Vajrayana meditation, often associated with the concept of "vajra," representing a diamond or thunderbolt symbolizing indestructibility and transcendence.

The term "tummo" translates to "inner fire" in Tibetan. Meditation harnesses the body's internal heat or energy, leading to profound physical and spiritual transformation. The primary aim of tummo meditation is to awaken the natural inner heat, enabling the practitioner to generate intense warmth within their body even in freezing conditions.

In 2007, amidst the lush jungles of Bali, I stumbled upon something extraordinary during a profound meditation session. After each meditation, an incredible transformation would occur – my body would release overflowing amounts of sweat, a natural detoxification process that left my skin feeling as soft as a baby's. The once prominent pores vanished, leaving my face glowing with youthful radiance. Even the gentlest breeze felt refined and sensational against my skin. This remarkable journey is one I'm eager to share with you.

Sitting on a rustic mat in the lotus position, surrounded by crawling insects, some potentially deadly, I paid no heed to their presence. I focused on connecting with the Earth and the cosmic sun through the central channel running along my spine.

Sitting in this posture for some time, I noticed a circle of ants forming around me as if they could sense my energy or vibration. They circled me without touching, a curious and awe-inspiring sight.

Upon closing my eyes to continue my meditation, I suddenly caught the scent of incense. At first, I thought it was a mere figment of my imagination. However, when I opened my eyes again, I found a Balinese girl sitting beside me prayerfully, holding incense sticks, despite no one else in the area. Such occurrences are rare in the jungle. My energy had been sensed and amplified through her prayer. Intriguing indeed!

I've also meditated in various public places, witnessing the environment drastically change around me. It's a fascinating experiment for those open to such experiences. Upon returning to the same spot the following day, I encountered an invisible barrier—a residual energy field from my previous meditation. It is a captivating realization, to say the least.

Consistently, after these profound meditations, the cleansing process would begin again, inducing sweating and leaving my skin silky-smooth. My pores became so refined that my facial skin felt like silk. Contrary to common belief, blushing isn't confined to youth alone; it can occur when facial skin is relaxed, allowing energy to flow freely. While this meditation softens the skin, resulting in a younger appearance, it is, in essence, a natural detoxification method. It proves to be highly effective against acne, enlarged pores, and damaged skin.

Let's start with the meditation:

1. **Positioning**: Find a comfortable seat, ensuring your spine is erect. Ground your base, feeling the Earth beneath

you. Soften the features of your face, allowing any tension to melt away.

2. **Breathing Pattern**: Gently inhale through your nose, deepening the air into your lower abdomen. Visualize this breath as a warm energy. Exhale softly, releasing this warmth through both your nose and the pores of your face, always keeping your facial muscles at ease.

3. **Circulating Warmth**: On your next inhalation, draw warmth through the pores of your face, guiding it into your lower abdomen. As you exhale, visualize this warmth radiating from your lower stomach and facial pores. Embrace any tingling sensations on your face; this could be an early sign of perspiration. Keep your face serene and relaxed.

4. **Visualization**: Imagine this warm energy flowing seamlessly with each inhale and exhale, circulating between

your face and abdomen. If you sense any tingling on your face as you breathe, acknowledge it — this indicates that perspiration might be beginning. It's essential to remain in tune with these sensations, recognizing the warmth on your face.

5. **Expanding the Flow**: Gradually, envision this warmth extending from your facial pores to encompass the pores of your entire body. Picture your skin like a sponge, absorbing and releasing heat with each breath. As you continue, imagine droplets forming and emerging from your pores, invigorating your body. This imagery is akin to signaling your body, guiding its response.

6. **Culmination**: Once you've grasped this visualization and sensation, continue the rhythmic breathing and warmth circulation until you feel it's

the right moment to wrap up the meditation.

Note: For beginners or to enhance this meditation, consider practicing in a warm setting like a bath, shower, sauna, or near a heater. Remember to stay hydrated, sipping water or tea to support the process.

You might not sweat at first, but that's perfectly fine. Even so, you'll find your skin becoming softer and toxins being released. The next time will be easier. In essence, detoxification has long been celebrated for its profound impact on physical, mental, and spiritual health. Whether through dietary changes or meditation methods like tummo, there are numerous ways to bolster the body's innate ability to cleanse and reestablish balance. Adopting detox practices can rejuvenate and invigorate us, propelling us to embrace life at its peak.

Chapter 13: Natural Facelifting, Lip Augmentation, and Bodyshaping

We previously discussed appearance, where beauty can be a status symbol in fashion, entertainment, cosmetics, social media, influencer culture, and high-end lifestyle brands. Although our physical appearances can play a significant role in society, this self-help book intends to self-improve ourselves through life force energy, including our physical appearance. When reflecting on my life, I use the Natural Facelift method because it makes me feel more comfortable, not necessarily to impress others. Ultimately, the external world is merely a reflection of our inner world. When I use the Natural Facelift method and receive feedback from the outside world or when looking in the mirror, it serves as confirmation. We also explored the "observed reality" theme, where consciousness can influence our environment and ourselves. We discussed that prolonged stress blocks life force energy, resulting in disease-related symptoms and signs of aging. By cultivating life force, we can reverse the aging process, as is possible with the Natural Facelift method.

Natural Facelifting differs from cosmetic surgical procedures that aim to rejuvenate and tighten the face's appearance. The same effect can be achieved through the Natural Facelift method by cultivating life force energy, reducing wrinkles, tightening the skin, and restoring a youthful look to the face. I began experimenting with this method around 18/19 when I noticed my first signs of wrinkles, particularly on my forehead. Wrinkles are tension fields around the face, which we can relax to make them disappear. However, relaxation alone is not enough; it becomes essential when working with life force energy. It is the combination of life force and facial relaxation. When we activate this energy in our face and relax our facial muscles, we can quickly feel the skin tightening, similar to the effect of stimulating collagen through life force. I have seen myself age in front of the mirror, but fortunately, I have always managed to reverse it by cultivating life force energy. A mirror can be a valuable tool when using the Natural Facelift method. First, we must understand that wrinkles are nothing more than tension fields around the face, often habitual for our facial expressions. The second point is recognizing whether we can feel or perceive these tensions in our faces. If we cannot, then standing in front of the mirror might help. Facial tensions can manifest as forehead wrinkles, frown lines, crow's feet, laugh lines, marionette lines, etc. Once we observe them, can we feel these tensions in our faces? If so, relax them and activate the life force energy in the face, as we practiced, for example, with the palm chakras. The face also has chakras that facilitate the energy flow, making the facial skin more elastic. Chakras are energy vortexes fully operating on life force energy. We only need to set our intention and keep our concentration focused. These pressure points are located between the eyebrows, just above the bridge of the nose, inside the eyebrows, along the nose bridge, at both sides of the nostrils, where the cheeks begin, just below each eye's pupil, on the bone around the eye sockets, and on the sides of the eyebrows where crow's feet may appear. The face undergoes a rejuvenating process by activating the energy at these points. We can also place our fingertips on these points, as our fingertips contain chakras that facilitate energy, akin to laser beams, during healing work.

Once we can feel the life force energy in our face by simply activating it, simultaneously relaxing the facial tensions, and maintaining our focus throughout the day, we will notice the skin tightening, resulting in a more youthful appearance. It is genuinely straightforward once you know how to do it. However, I recommend mastering the Natural Detox described in the previous chapter for the best results. Natural Detox ensures the skin becomes super fine and soft, whereas Natural Facelifting helps wrinkles disappear from the face and tighten the skin. Another crucial aspect is to keep the face relaxed even after the session. We might be accustomed to expressing ourselves through facial expressions (mimicry), but I advise against it because it can cause us to pick up and reinforce facial tensions. This might be a challenge for many people. People with fillers or Botox may show less mimicry, and no one seems to mind. In some cultures, such as Japan and other Asian countries, people use less mimicry and look less aged later in life. In Japanese culture, subtle and reserved mimicry is often considered more appropriate than exuberant facial expressions. Learning to communicate with less mimicry is fine; no one will mind it. By reducing our mimicry, wrinkles fade away, and the skin tightens when life force energy is active. If we find cultivating life force energy in the face challenging, I recommend starting with a facial massage or Faceyoga to relieve tension.

Furthermore, consistency is key when practicing the Natural Facelift method. Regular sessions will yield better results over time. As we become more attuned to our life force energy and facial tensions, we develop a greater awareness of maintaining a youthful appearance.

It is essential to remember that Natural Facelifting is not merely about achieving a wrinkle-free face or conforming to societal beauty standards. Instead, it is a holistic approach to inner and outer well-being. By cultivating life force energy and promoting relaxation, we enhance our physical appearance and foster overall health and balance.

Incorporating the Natural Facelift method into our daily routine can become a mindful and transformative practice. As we focus on our life force energy and facial expressions, we deepen our connection with ourselves and the world around us. This self-awareness and self-care can lead to increased self-confidence and a positive outlook on life.

In cultures where people use less mimicry, like Japan and other Asian countries, emphasizing inner harmony and self-discipline can contribute to a more balanced and youthful appearance as individuals age gracefully.

As we continue our journey of self-improvement and self-discovery, let us embrace the power of life force energy and the Natural Facelift method to radiate our inner vitality and beauty. Remember, this is not a quick-fix solution per se but a lifelong practice that aligns our inner and outer selves, allowing us to embrace the passage of time with grace and authenticity.

In conclusion, Natural Facelifting goes beyond skin-deep aesthetics and allows us to harmonize our mind, body, and spirit. We can witness the transformative power of our own vitality by harnessing the life force energy within us and relaxing our facial tensions. So, let us embark on this journey of self-care, self-awareness, and rejuvenation to unlock the true potential of our inner beauty and well-being.

13.1 Natural Lip Augmentation

I have always been a curious experimenter regarding energy and physical transformation. In my younger years, I often played with altering the size of my lips using the life force. It happened spontaneously at first. I recall that sometimes my lips would turn red due to the energy, leading people to ask if I was wearing lipstick. I was always surprised by their questions until I looked in the mirror. It was fascinating to see my lips turn vivid red without any lipstick. Although my lips were already decent-sized, I couldn't help but wonder what would happen if I made them even more significant.

Once, I made them so big that they looked disproportionate to the rest of my face, which was quite an unusual sight, prompting me to quickly return them to standard size. You're probably thinking, "Wait, did the author just talk about changing the size of his lips?" Yes, he did! Working with life force energy is a fascinating realm with many discoveries yet to be made. Let's take a closer look at the structure of the lips: they consist of different layers. The outermost layer, the epidermis, is thinner than in other parts of the body, making the lips less protected against UV radiation and dehydration. Beneath the epidermis lies the dermis, which is thicker and contains collagen and elastin fibers, providing the lips with firmness and elasticity. The innermost layer, the mucous membrane, is similar to the mucous membrane found in other parts of the mouth and is rich in blood vessels, giving the lips their reddish or pinkish color. Around the lips, various muscles play a crucial role in mouth and lip movement. Moreover, the lips are exposed due to a high density of sensory nerves, making them responsive to touch, temperature, and pressure, which is why kissing is such a pleasurable experience.

The lip border is responsible for increasing or decreasing lip size. We can enlarge the lips by channeling life force energy and infusing it into the lip border while keeping it relaxed. Initially, the lip border will expand and darken in color, indicating that the lips are enlarging. At this stage, our lips might feel different, experiencing tingling or mild dryness. Once again, we can use a mirror to observe the status of our lips.

Conversely, if we want smaller lips, we exert concentrated pressure on the lip border as if creating a tension field that causes our lips to shrink. We can liken the lips to the analogy of a balloon that can be inflated or deflated. The tension field around the lip border facilitates lip reduction.

I recall the icy winter periods when lips could crack from the cold and become very dry. People tend to apply lip balm to prevent this. However, I discovered that when we relax our lips during such moments, a strange feeling arises due to a mucous membrane on the lips. This sensation leads us to wipe off the lips, even though the mucous membrane prevents them from drying out. It's as if we have an inbuilt mechanism against dry lips. During winter, it can be helpful to relax the lips and allow the natural lipid layer to form. This lipid layer is far superior to lip balm because it contains our unique DNA, enabling rapid healing of any cracks caused by dehydration, which no ointment could achieve. I noticed that this lipid layer often appears black, and although I can't explain the color, I can certainly attest to its effectiveness. However, the formation of this lipid layer only occurs when I allow it through some sort of meditation. We can do so much more with our bodies than we realize.

I am not as preoccupied with changing the size of my lips anymore, but sharing this knowledge is essential for those who want to take it further.

Like Natural Facelifting, where facial skin can be tightened using life force energy, we can modify our lips through Natural Lip Augmentation. Let me repeat: we can alter our lips by relaxing the lip border and activating or multiplying the life force energy, causing the lips to appear plumper as if inflated.

The process of Natural Lip Augmentation is a unique and personal journey for each individual. It requires a deep understanding of one's energy and the ability to connect profoundly. Through focused intention and practice, one can learn to manipulate the flow of life force energy to achieve the desired lip size and appearance changes.

As with any energy work, it is crucial to approach Natural Lip Augmentation with mindfulness for the body's natural balance. Working with the lip border and its subtle energies demands a gentle touch and a patient attitude. Moreover, Natural Lip Augmentation is not about conforming to societal beauty standards or seeking approval from others. It is an empowering practice that allows individuals to embrace their unique features and explore their self-expression. The focus should be on enhancing one's natural beauty, not striving for an unrealistic or artificial appearance.

In addition to the physical changes, Natural Lip Augmentation can positively affect one's emotional and energetic well-being. By harmonizing and balancing the energies within the lip area, individuals may experience a newfound sense of confidence, self-acceptance, and connection to their inner selves.

As this practice gains recognition and interest. Proper guidance and training from experienced practitioners can help ensure that individuals engage in Natural Lip Augmentation.

Furthermore, embracing the concept of Natural Lip Augmentation opens the door to a broader understanding of the body-mind connection and the limitless possibilities of energy work. It encourages exploration, not only in the realm of physical appearance but also in various aspects of personal growth and transformation.

As more individuals become aware of the potential of Natural Lip Augmentation, the field of energy-based practices will likely expand, leading to further research and a deeper understanding of the human body's energetic nature.

In conclusion, Natural Lip Augmentation is a fascinating journey that explores the intersection of energy and physical form. It empowers individuals to connect with their innate life force energy and harness it to naturally enhance their lips' appearance.

13.2 Bodyshaping

We extensively discussed the benefits of life energy, which can have positive implications for the body and mind. We also delved into Natural Facelifting through life force cultivation to physically rejuvenate the face. Similarly, body shaping can be achieved through life force energy and intention. Depending on the purpose for which this energy is employed, it can serve various objectives, given its inherent universality. There is much more to discover in this realm, and it's something that we can all contribute to. I envision a future where society at large harnesses the potential of life force energy, akin to how yoga gained widespread recognition in the past. The emergence of yoga studios was reminiscent of mushrooms sprouting from the ground, and nowadays, almost everyone is familiar with yoga. In contrast, Bodyshaping is relatively unexplored—an area I delved into years ago as I pursued further development and explored the possibilities of life force energy.

"Bodyshaping" is a term I adopted because it allows us to sculpt our bodies using energy as the foundation. Unlike conventional gym workouts that rely on weights, this approach emphasizes stimulating muscles through controlled tension, building the life force while relaxing the body simultaneously, excluding using weights. In the second part, we venture into body shaping without physical movement. Regrettably, I can't delve into the specifics of the first part here, as it involves visual elements and would be too detailed for this format. Much like yoga, body shaping stands on its own as a practice. There's potential for me to offer lessons, online workshops, or courses in the future. However, I can share the second part of the practice with more advanced practitioners of life force energy.

While life force energy is inherently potent, it takes on a symbiotic dimension when actively utilized. This synergy leads to an upgrade in capabilities, effectively turning life force energy into a tool. In a previous chapter, we discussed the concept of the Life Force Body, where energy flows throughout the entire body and potentially optimizes it. With Bodyshaping, we infuse our intentions into the process of shaping the body, as if directing the life force energy through our minds. Interestingly, this prompts individual muscles to autonomously contract, resembling the effects of devices like an "electrostimulation" or "electrical muscle stimulator" (EMS). EMS devices use electrical impulses to induce muscle contractions, aiding muscle development, rehabilitation, and physical therapy. This effect can also be achieved naturally without the aid of a device.

I recall a time in my youth, around 17, when I playfully pondered the idea of having abdominal muscles while looking in the mirror. I lay on my bed for about five minutes while casually setting my intention. Upon attempting to stand, I found myself unable to do so due to sudden muscle soreness, mainly in my abdominal area. Surprisingly, I now had a set of well-defined abdominal muscles in just five minutes! This experience showcased the potential of sculpting the body through energy. This phenomenon reminds me of the concept of physical training and mental visualization within the context of athletic performance.

Such studies often explore the role of mental preparation in enhancing performance and how it relates to traditional physical training.

In a hypothetical experiment, two participants would be involved: one group undergoing physical training to prepare for a sports competition and another group engaging in mental visualization of the competition and successful performance without experiencing physical activity.

The overarching aim of the experiment would be to determine whether mental visualization, without actual physical training, could yield similar or even superior performance compared to traditional physical exercise alone. Interestingly, some participants who focused on mental visualization also experienced increased muscle mass.

This phenomenon raises intriguing parallels with harnessing the mind-body connection to enhance physical capabilities. It underscores the powerful interplay between mental intention, energy, and the physical body. Just as my experience revealed the rapid transformation of muscle appearance through focused purpose, numerous sports psychology and performance enhancement studies explore the potential of mental training alongside or even physical exercise.

Instead of solely relying on traditional training methods, imagine a scenario where athletes incorporate intensive mental visualization techniques into their regimens. This mental rehearsal vividly imagines successful performances, skill execution, and desired physical outcomes. The goal is to stimulate the neural pathways associated with physical movement and muscle engagement, thus priming the body for optimal execution during competition.

Research suggests that mental visualization can enhance muscle activation, improve motor coordination, and even expedite muscle growth in some instances. The neural signals generated during vivid mental imagery activate similar brain regions as physical execution, bridging the gap between mind and body.

Exercise:

1. Begin by finding a comfortable sitting position, ensuring your Life Force Body is fully activated.
2. While maintaining a relaxed state, focus on amplifying the energy coursing through your muscles.
3. Set a clear intention for muscle growth, allowing yourself to truly connect with and feel this transformational process. Patience is critical during this phase.

4. Pay attention to the subtle movements of your muscles. As they move independently, it's a sign that your body is adjusting and the Bodyshaping process is underway.

Additionally, utilizing life force energy as a catalyst for Bodyshaping adds another layer of depth to the conversation. Practitioners may facilitate targeted muscle growth and sculpting by aligning intention, focus, and energy. This process illustrates the intricate interplay between consciousness and the physical form, echoing age-old philosophical and spiritual ideologies.

While physical training remains indispensable for building strength, endurance, and overall fitness, integrating mental visualization and life force energy manipulation introduces a fascinating dimension. It questions the boundaries of our potential and invites us to explore the untapped capacities of the human mind and body.

As sports science, psychology, and holistic wellness continue to converge, the concept of Bodyshaping through energy and intention is a testament to how our thoughts and energies can shape our physical reality. This fusion of ancient wisdom and contemporary understanding underscores the uncharted territories that lie ahead for humanity's exploration of mind, body, and consciousness.

Body Shaping through life force energy and intention exemplifies the intricate connection between mental focus, energetic influence, and physical transformation. It prompts us to reconsider the boundaries of possibility and encourages us to explore the synergies between the life force, mind, and body, ultimately unveiling new frontiers in human potential.

Chapter 14: Life Force, Trauma, the Central Channel, Palm Chakras and Manifestation

I remember a time when "The Secret" suddenly became very popular. For those unfamiliar, "The Secret" is about shaping your life through intention and visualization. However, the downside of "The Secret" is that it doesn't mention that if we have a lot of unresolved traumas, we may not be able to manifest our dream life effectively. Have you ever noticed that some people have many opportunities available while others seem to experience constant misfortune, regardless of their mindset or manifesting actions?

I can relate to this because I used to share it until I resolved my traumas, which completely transformed my reality.

So, what is a trauma? Trauma is a psychological response to a shocking or impactful event that can seriously disrupt someone's emotional well-being. Traumatic events can include physical violence, sexual abuse, serious accidents, natural disasters, war, loss of a loved one, and other situations that someone finds highly stressful. Trauma can also result from repeated exposure to harmful circumstances, such as prolonged abuse or chronic stress.

In essence, trauma is a low-energy form stored in the body. When we carry trauma for too long, it can, from a holistic perspective, develop into illness. Metaphysically, unresolved trauma can repeat in our lives because we attract people and related situations due to carrying it within us. The inner and outer worlds are interconnected. Traumas often come with associated tension fields that can block life energy in certain parts of the body. I believe eliminating traumas is crucial when shaping our lives through manifestation. Traumas can also cling to various beliefs, including:

1. Self-worth and self-esteem: Trauma can make someone feel unworthy or not good enough. This lack of self-worth can lead to unconscious self-sabotage and rejection of opportunities for life improvement.
2. Fear and negativity: Trauma can lead to constant anxiety, pessimism, and negative thoughts. These emotions and thoughts can hinder the manifestation of positive changes because they conflict with positive intentions.
3. Patterns of self-sabotage: People with unresolved traumas may unconsciously develop repeating patterns of self-sabotage. They may

attract situations that confirm their pain and negative beliefs, even when consciously trying to create positive changes.

4. Limiting beliefs: Trauma can result in deeply rooted limiting beliefs, such as "I don't deserve happiness" or "life is always hard." These beliefs can make it challenging to formulate positive intentions and believe they can become a reality.

In the Netherlands, the saying: "Doe maar gewoon 'normaal,' dan doe je al gek genoeg," translates to "Just be 'normal,' that's crazy enough." In other words, it suggests accepting "self-imposed limitations is okay.

The question is, what is considered normal? What people mean by average is living according to the standard, although what's considered normal can vary worldwide. Normal is relative. When I think about normal, I think about ethical norms and values. I think about how I can help myself and make the world a better place. Personally, I believe that everything is a reflection of our inner world. If there are things in our reality that we don't like, we should turn inward and examine what it represents within ourselves. Even things that happen in our existence that initially trigger resistance often have a reason behind them. I've spoken to many people who have experienced very challenging things, such as a serious illness, and they've ultimately become better people because of it. I've had incurable diseases since childhood, which led me to cultivate my life force and resolve them to pass on what I've learned. That same principle applies to traumas. I've experienced some intense things and have gone through deep valleys. Now, I help people with traumas simply by removing the stored emotional charge from their system, which allows them to manifest

297

better. I don't believe in 20 years of therapy or endlessly talking about your problems. Instead, I focus on extracting the issue's core, the trauma's stored energy or emotional charge. I believe that a significant portion of humanity is traumatized in some way. Therefore, it's logical that only a tiny percentage of people actually lead their dream lives. I always say that the first step is to energetically cleanse yourself, mainly when manifesting. If the inner and outer worlds are basically one and the same, purification is crucial; otherwise, we can't display what we genuinely want due to our traumas.

Understanding and healing trauma is a deeply personal and transformative journey. It involves facing the past, releasing emotional burdens, and rebuilding a sense of self-worth and empowerment. It's not about denying or ignoring the traumas we've experienced but acknowledging them and finding ways to heal. By doing so, we can break free from the patterns of self-sabotage and limiting beliefs that hold us back from manifesting the life we desire. It's a journey toward self-discovery, self-acceptance, and self-fulfillment.

14.1 The Central Channel and Manifestation

In another chapter, we discussed the Djed in ancient Egypt, the central channel. The pyramids are brimming with symbolism related to them, and I have personally explored one of these pyramids. They were used by hierophants, the high priests of their time. The hieroglyphs suggest spiritual wisdom, particularly the Djed, from which the word "djedhi" is derived, meaning "life force." Why is this symbol so significant, and why are the pyramids and temples in Egypt illustrated with it? The Djed serves as a bridge between the spiritual and earthly realms and implies superpowers latent within humans that can be cultivated through life energy practices, akin to the principles of Kundalini philosophy. The pyramids are energy generators that also have a spiritual function. I once envisioned that the pyramids would be repurposed at the dawn of a new era after the fall of governments as we know them today. In this vision, I saw enlightened masters and initiates collectively cultivating higher consciousness, with one enlightened master and disciple entering at a time to channel the power of the pyramid through the Djedh or central channel. The pyramid acts as a magnifying glass, focusing cosmic energy into the Earth. Hence, the point is most vital at the base of the pyramid. When someone with a high spiritual level or Djed meditates in a specific spot within the pyramid, it can result in Samadhi or nirvana, as the energy flows through the spine, activating all energy centers inside and outside the body. In my vision, the enlightened master guides their disciple through this process.

Why is this so important? The pyramids were built in an advanced civilization and a different era when people possessed profound wisdom. This might be difficult for many to grasp, but it is undeniable that the pyramids are a testament to a level of craftsmanship that cannot be replicated today. It all comes down to consciousness, something the people of the time understood well. Those who lack consciousness create chaos and a world of separation. The Djed, or the central channel through which life energy flows, also serves the function of manifestation.

In another chapter, we discussed hermetic principles and the relationship between the inner and outer worlds. We also delved into the chakra system. Each chakra is connected to or has a relationship with the external world. A malfunctioning chakra can hinder our flow in certain situations. For example, someone who needs to be grounded more often experiences financial problems. This is also observed in individuals who have a solid spiritual connection but struggle to drop themselves, consequently not achieving the financial freedom they desire. Being well-grounded but lacking a spiritual connection may prevent someone from attaining spiritual insight or intelligence. Both aspects are crucial for manifestation. We need grounding to physically manifest and wisdom to draw closer to the divine through the dimensions that lie vertically above us. We can channel the higher vibrations and create a paradise here on Earth. If we keep in touch with both sides. Visualization springs from the power of thought but requires an anchor point to manifest physically. Both elements are essential. The central channel through which life energy flows influences our manifestation. The solar plexus chakra in the body serves as an energetic storage place. It provides the drive to connect the corresponding actions to our visualization and manifestation when in balance.

Furthermore, the central channel, often likened to the Djed in ancient Egypt, plays a critical role in the art of manifestation. It serves as the conduit through which our life force energy flows, influencing our ability to shape our reality. Just as the pyramids stand as timeless symbols of profound wisdom and spiritual power, our own inner Djed holds the potential to unlock superhuman abilities within us.

14.2 Palm chakras and manifestation

Our palm chakras are in direct connection with the outside world. They form the energetic bridge between our inner world and external reality. Located in the center of our hands, these chakras are crucial in exchanging energy and information with the world around us. Like the other chakras in our body, the palm chakras have a specific function. They serve as receiving and transmitting stations for energetic impulses. When we open and activate our hand's palm chakras, we can establish active connections with people, objects, and situations. This is why practices like laying on hands, healing touch, and even art forms like pranic healing can be so effective. Our hands can channel and share energy. In the context of manifestation, palm chakras are particularly relevant. When we use our hands to touch, hold, create, or even make symbolic gestures, we send intention and energy into the world. These conscious actions can serve as powerful manifestation tools. It's as if we physically place our senses in the world, making them more tangible. Think of writing goals on paper, holding a crystal during meditation, or giving a loving hug. In all these cases, we use our palm chakras to amplify our intentions and transmit energy. These actions can accelerate and strengthen the manifestation processes.

Furthermore, our hands also serve as instruments for receiving signals and energies from the outside world. They can pick up subtle information and provide us with intuitive insights. For example, we may instinctively feel we can trust someone through their handshake. To fully harness the potential of palm chakras in the manifestation process, it is essential to be aware of what we do with our hands and the intentions we transmit through them. By activating our hands and seeing them as powerful tools for conscious creation, we can further develop our manifestation skills and enhance our ability to shape our reality.

Our palm chakras are gateways between our inner and external worlds, essential to our spiritual growth and manifestation processes. Treating these chakras with respect and awareness is crucial to optimizing their powerful capabilities. In addition to physical touch, we can use the life force energy in our palm chakras to set intentions. Let us imagine having a stack of paper money in our hands; how does this feel? If we put the money away, can we still generate the cash energy in your palm chakra we felt before? If so, play with it regularly and be prepared to be surprised in the coming times. If not, keep practicing until you master it. In fact, you can do this with anything, such as a specific touch from someone or any object. This way, you can also manifest by channeling life force energy into the palm chakras of any entity, person, or situation.

Consider the scenario of holding paper money in your hand. The sensation you feel is not just about the physical texture of the money; it's also about the energy associated with it. Cash carries a significant energetic charge in our society linked to value, exchange, and abundance. By feeling this energy in your palm chakra, you're tapping into the collective consciousness and beliefs about money.

Now, as you put the money away and practice generating that same energy in your palm chakra without the physical object, you're disconnecting from the material form and accessing the pure life force energy that underlies it. This is a crucial step in conscious manifestation. You're learning to work with the essence of things rather than being limited by their physical presence.

As you become more proficient at generating and manipulating this energy in your palm chakras, you can apply it to various aspects of your life. For instance:

1. Relationships: When meeting
   someone new or interacting with
   loved ones, channel positive, loving,
   and harmonious energy through your
   palm chakras. This can help
   strengthen connections and create
   more fulfilling relationships.
2. Creativity: If you're an artist or a
   creative individual, use your palm
   chakras to infuse your work with your
   unique energy and intention. This can
   enhance the impact and resonance of
   your creations.
3. Healing: When someone you care
   about needs healing or comfort, direct
   healing energy through your hands.
   You can do this through focused
   intention through touch or even from
   a distance.
4. Goals and Intentions: Before setting
   out to achieve a specific purpose, use
   your palm chakras to charge it with
   intention and positive energy. This

amplifies your efforts and aligns you more closely with your desired outcomes.

5. Environmental Influence: Channeling energy into your surroundings, whether your home, workspace, or even a public place, can help create an atmosphere conducive to your goals and intentions.

Remember that manifesting with your palm chakras is a skill that can be refined over time. The more you practice and cultivate awareness of your palm chakras, the more adept you'll become at using them as tools for conscious creation. Trust in the power of your palm chakras to bridge the gap between your inner intentions and the external world, and watch as your desires begin to take shape in your reality with the life force.